SPRING 2020 FASHION ISSUE:

CABIN IN THE WOODS - PHOTO STORY BY MAXWELL ALEXANDER
P.3

A HISTORIC HUDSON VALLEY FARMHOUSE REINVENTED BY DUNCAN AVENUE DESIGN STUDIO
P.18

#SPRINGFASHION COVER STORY BY HELENA PALAZZI
P.26

HEALTHY SKIN NEVER GOES OUT OF STYLE - INTERVIEW WITH DR. BROOKE BAIR, DO
P.36

SPRING FASHION IN THE HUDSON VALLEY

PHOTO STORY BY **HELENA PALAZZI**
P.26

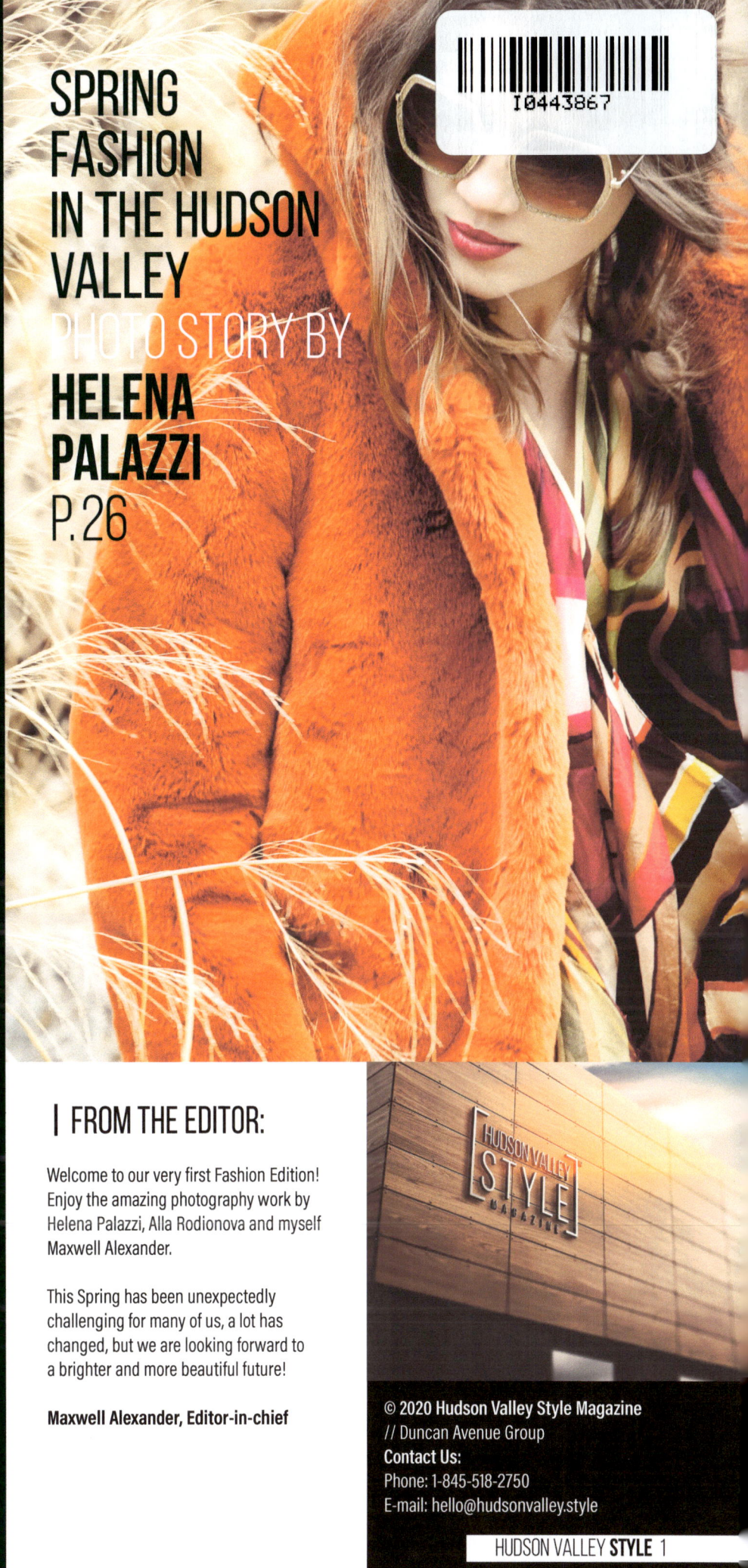

| FROM THE EDITOR:

Welcome to our very first Fashion Edition! Enjoy the amazing photography work by Helena Palazzi, Alla Rodionova and myself Maxwell Alexander.

This Spring has been unexpectedly challenging for many of us, a lot has changed, but we are looking forward to a brighter and more beautiful future!

Maxwell Alexander, Editor-in-chief

© 2020 Hudson Valley Style Magazine // Duncan Avenue Group
Contact Us:
Phone: 1-845-518-2750
E-mail: hello@hudsonvalley.style

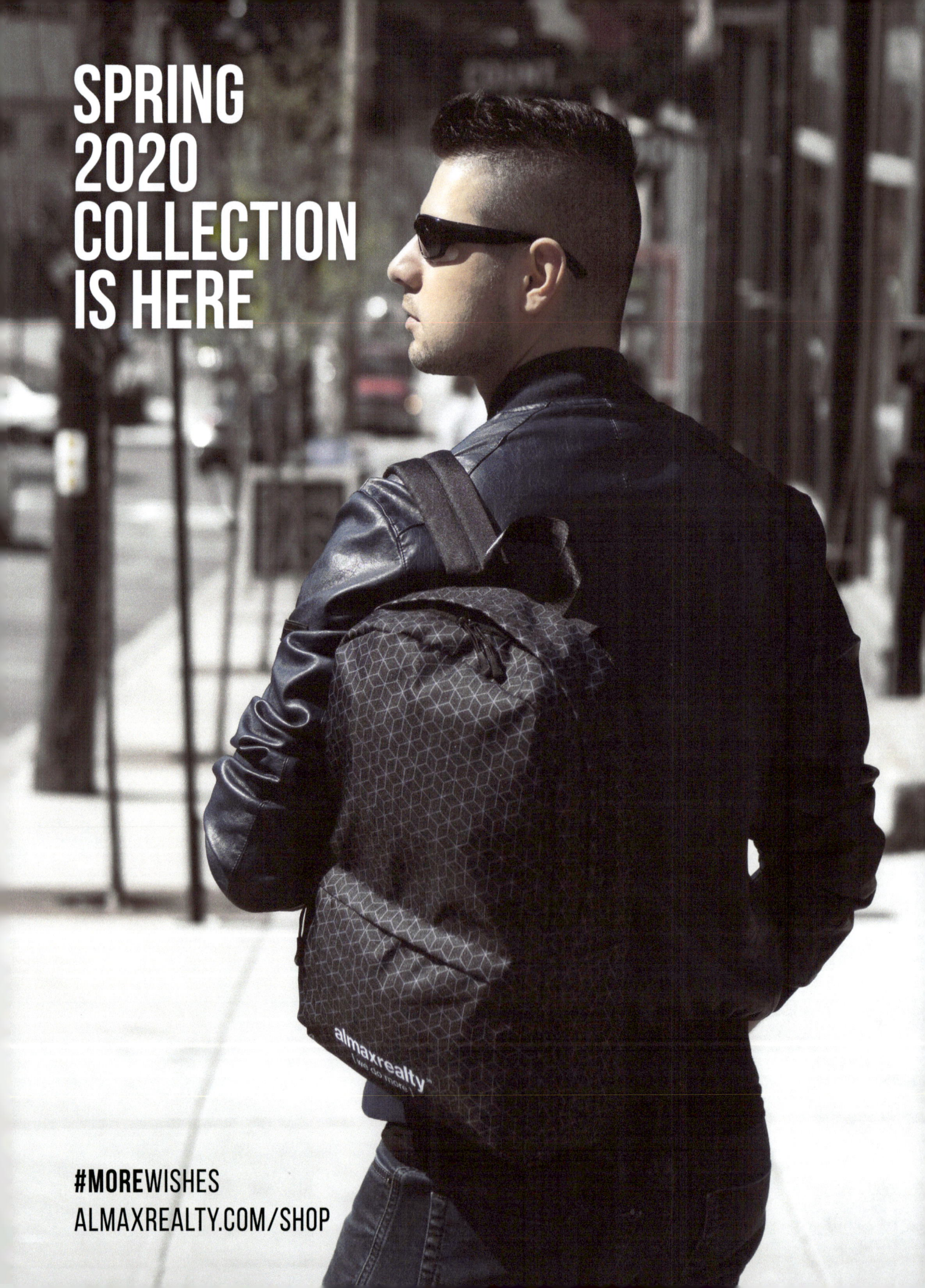

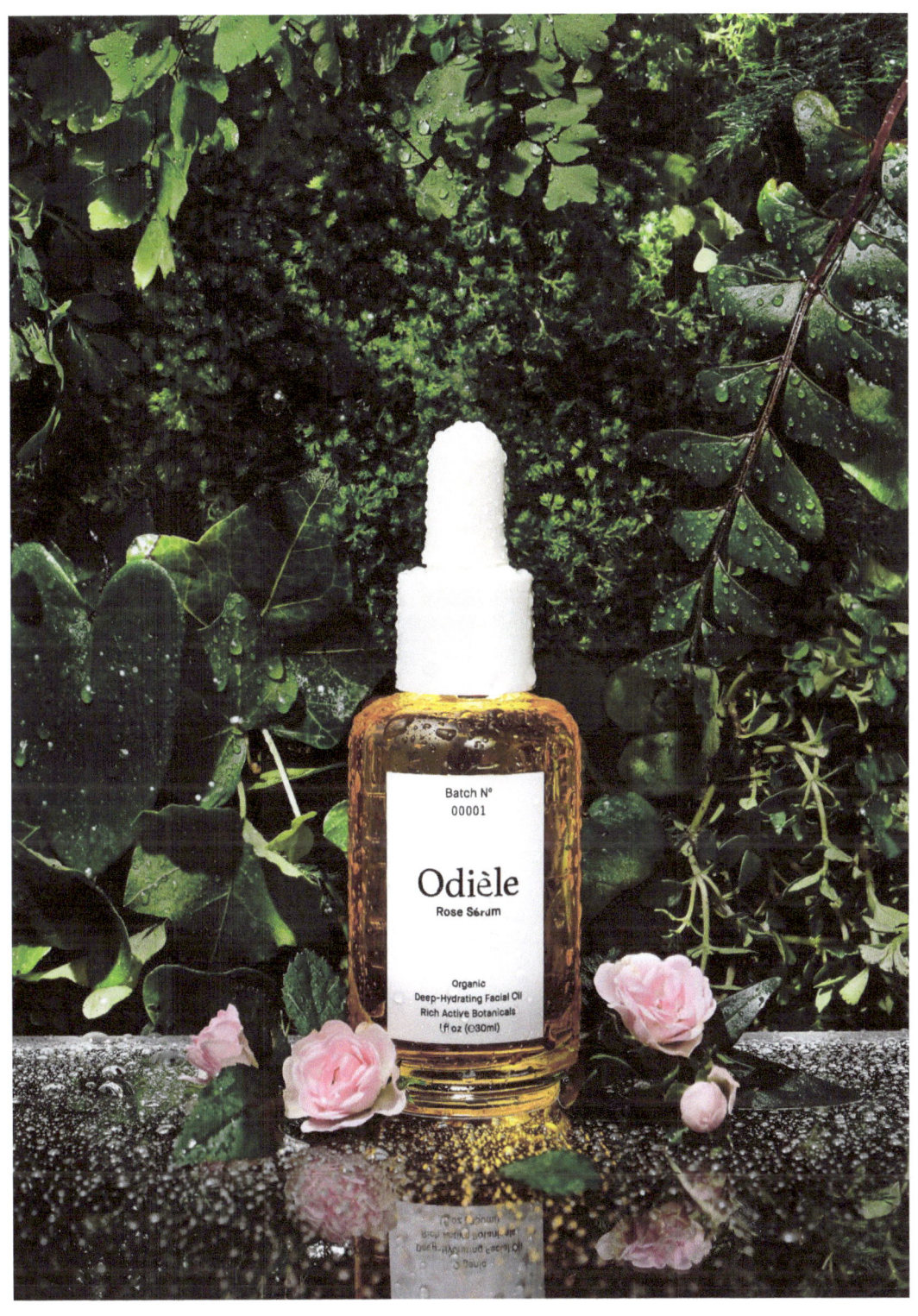

French Indulgence - Effortless, Effective, and Dripping Luxury.
odiele.com

FRESH AIR, INSPIRING DESIGN, WARMTH & COMFORT...
MAITOPIA PHOTO STORY BY MAXWELL ALEXANDER

Escape the craziness for a few days and keep a healthy distance from the rest of the World in Maitopia, Hudson Valley's hidden modern rustic gem in the middle of the woods in Red Hook, New York.

This beautifully designed passive glass & wood modern cabin offers elegant details and the warmth that only an upstate energy-efficient retreat could. With a soaking egg tub, fires at every turn and a year-round hot pool you will fall in love with the place and the towns nearby.

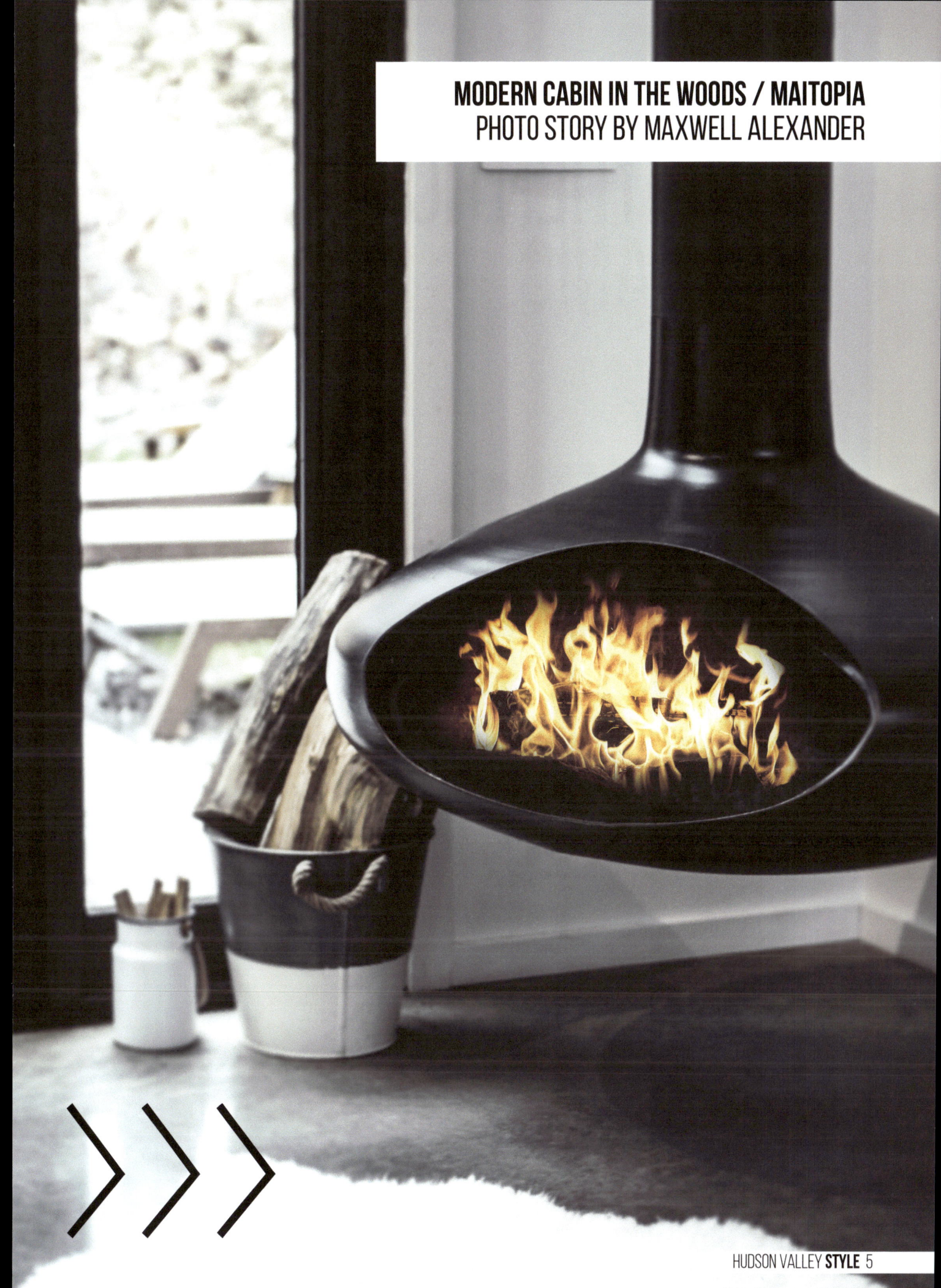

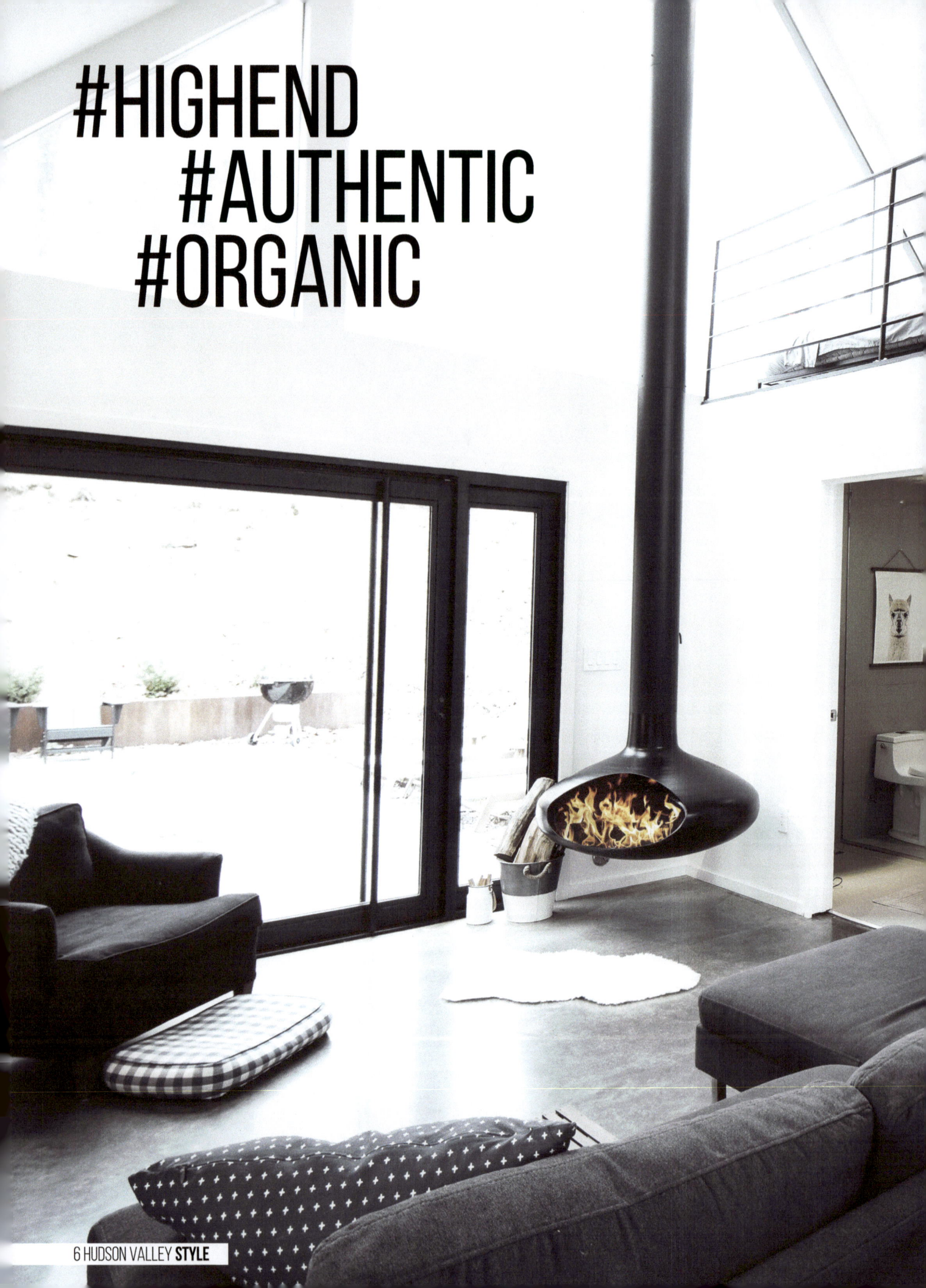

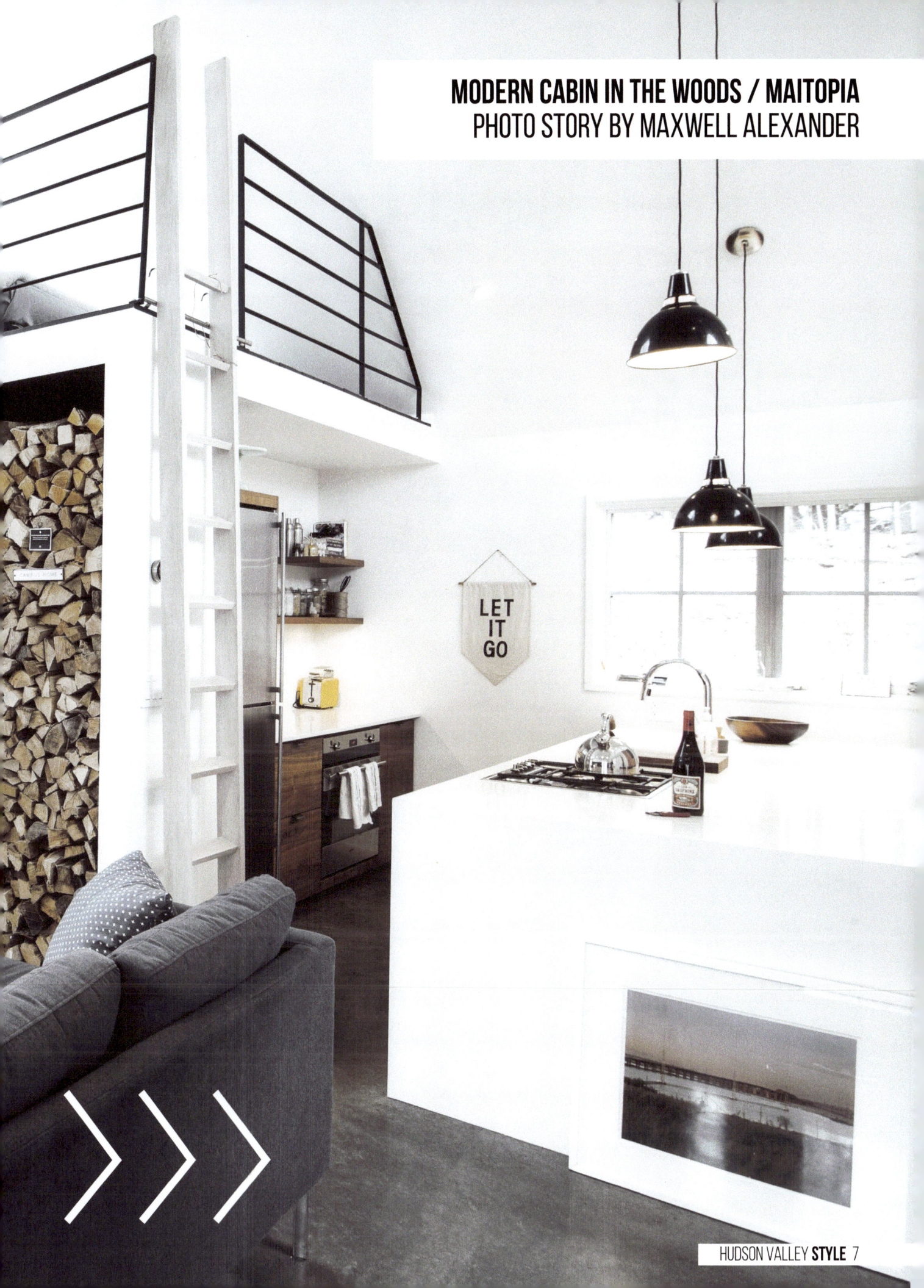

MODERN CABIN IN THE WOODS / MAITOPIA
PHOTO STORY BY MAXWELL ALEXANDER

#STYLE #DESIGN #HUDSONVALLEY

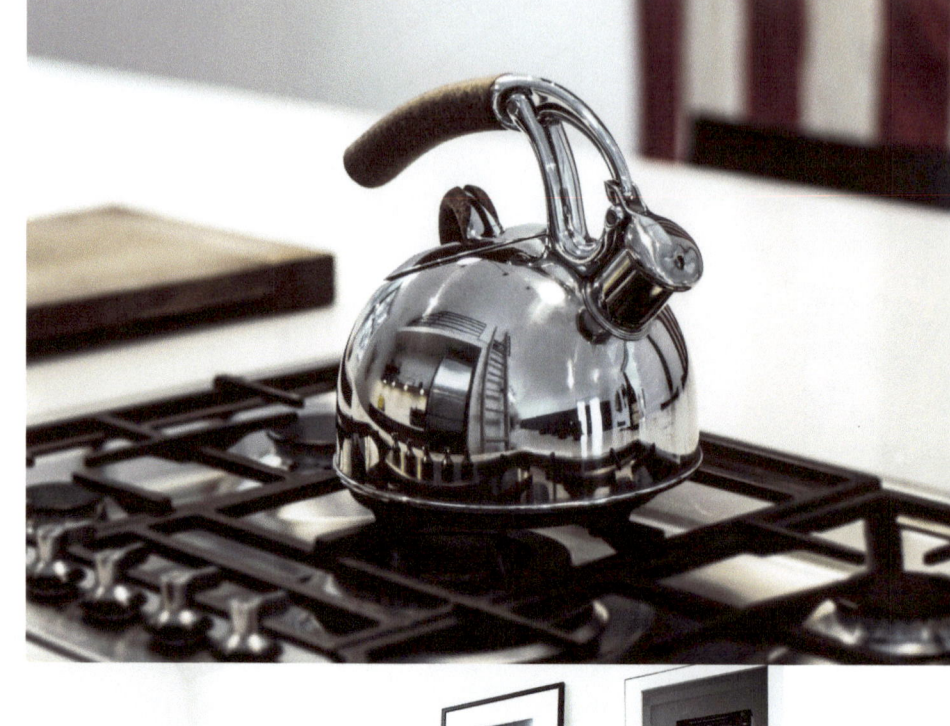

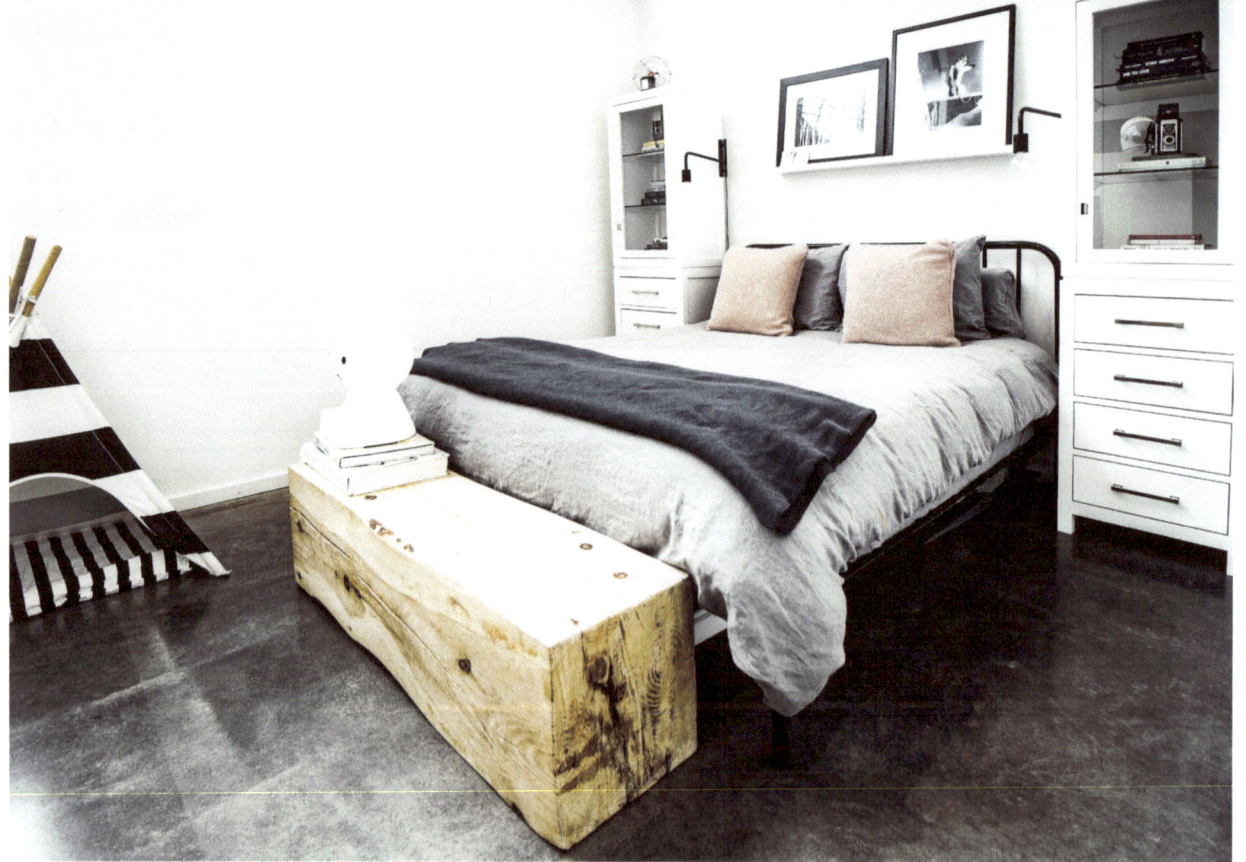

MODERN CABIN IN THE WOODS / MAITOPIA
PHOTO STORY BY MAXWELL ALEXANDER

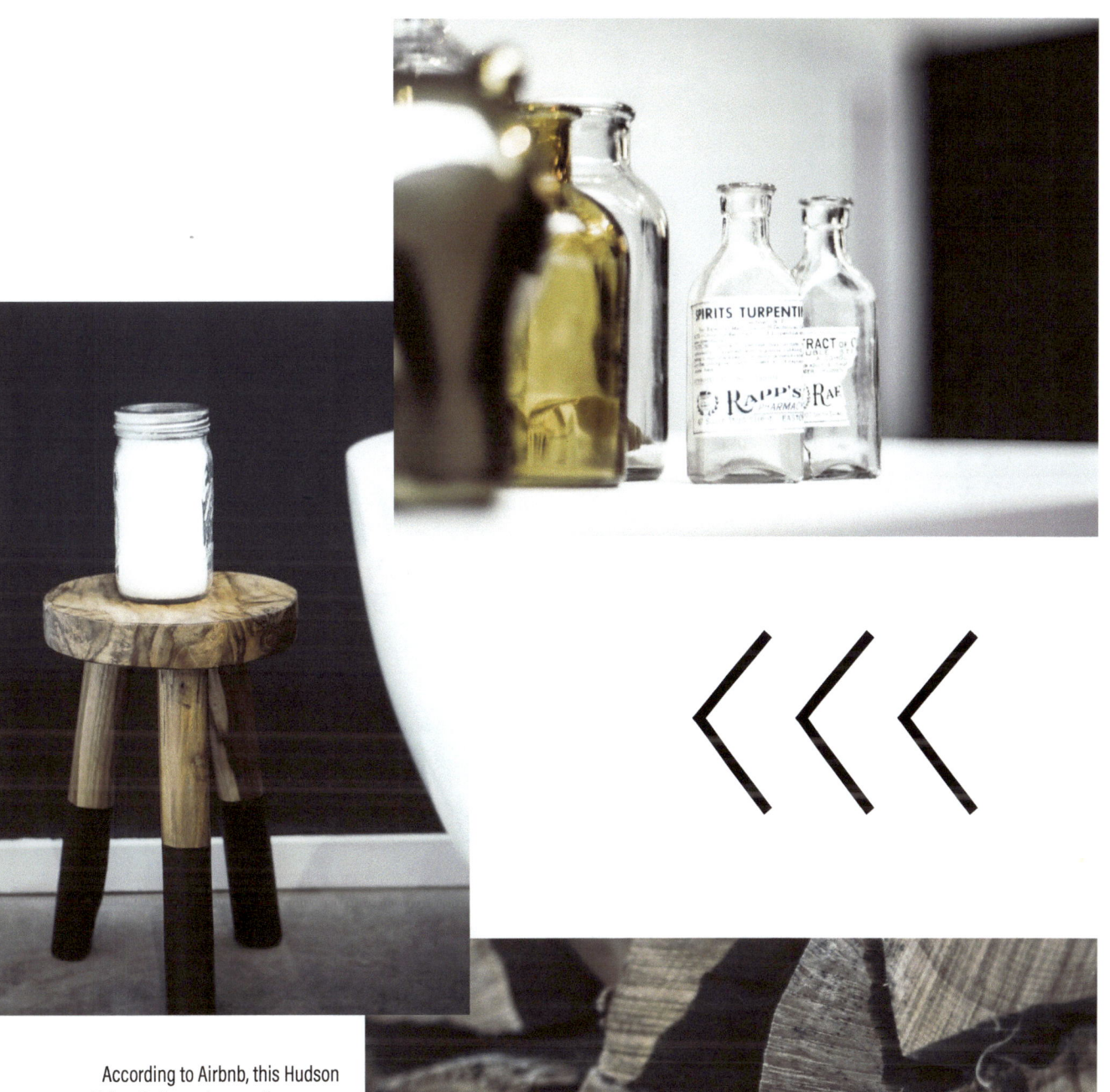

According to Airbnb, this Hudson Valley Style modern rustic energy-efficient retreat is getting a lot of attention recently, so check them on the platform in Rhinebeck, NY!

SUMMER PARADISE IN THE HUDSON VALLEY

**▎PHOTO STORY
BY MAXWELL ALEXANDER**

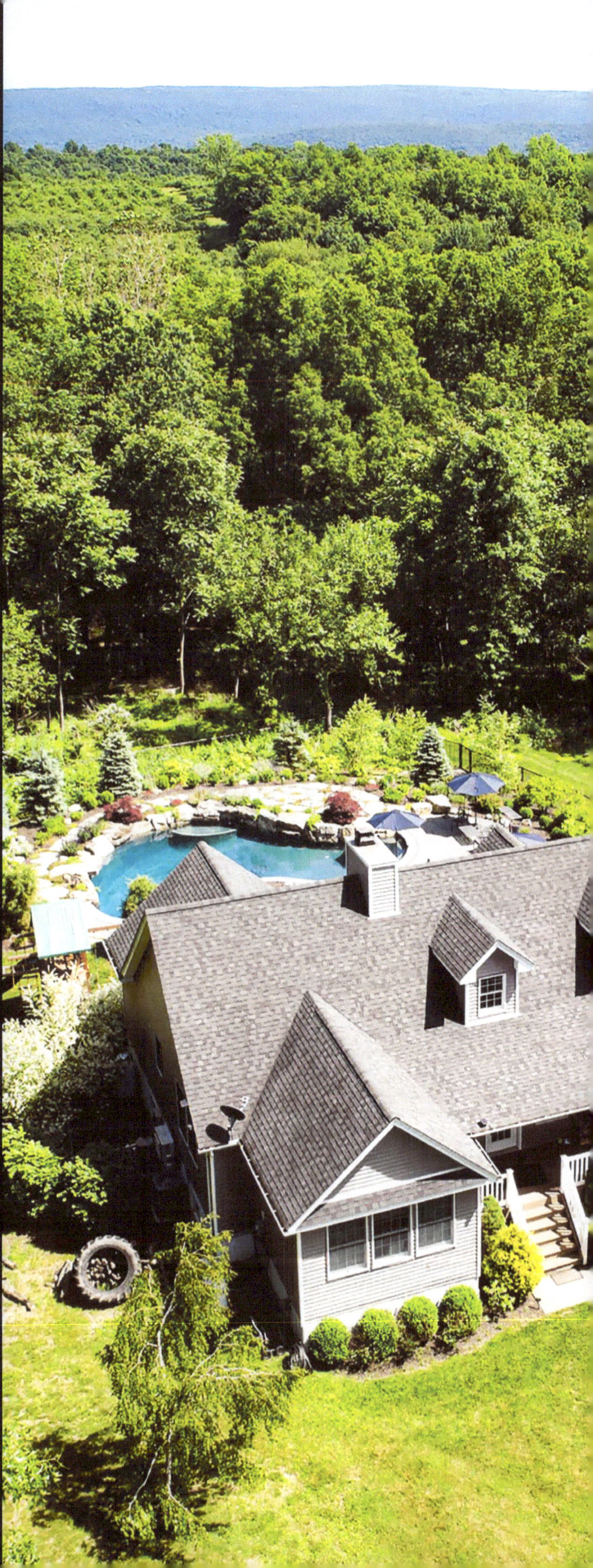

This photoshoot literally took more than 6 months to accomplish, just because summer is not a permanent thing in the Hudson Valley. In fact, I know a lot of people who weather the winter months in warmer climates such as Florida in the US or Caribbean Islands for those who are even luckier.

Well, for those who can still bear the snow and frigid temperatures here in the Modern Rustic Capital of the World, we can only dream of the warmer weather, so please enjoy this warm and fuzzy photo story from Rock Tavern, New York!

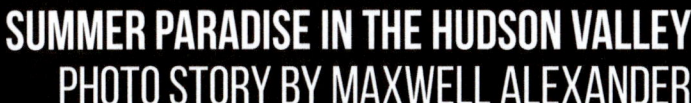

SUMMER PARADISE IN THE HUDSON VALLEY
PHOTO STORY BY MAXWELL ALEXANDER

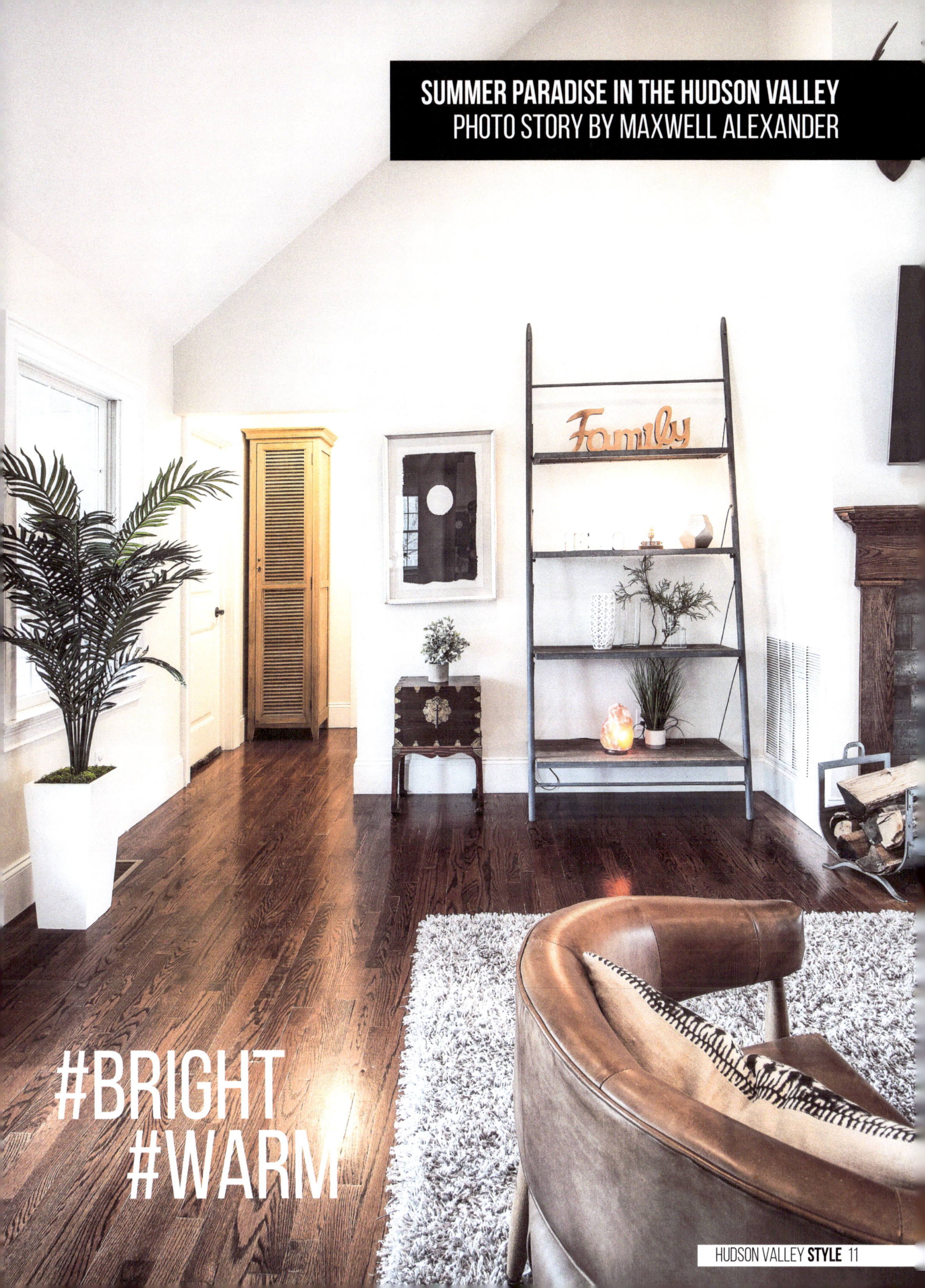

#BRIGHT
#WARM

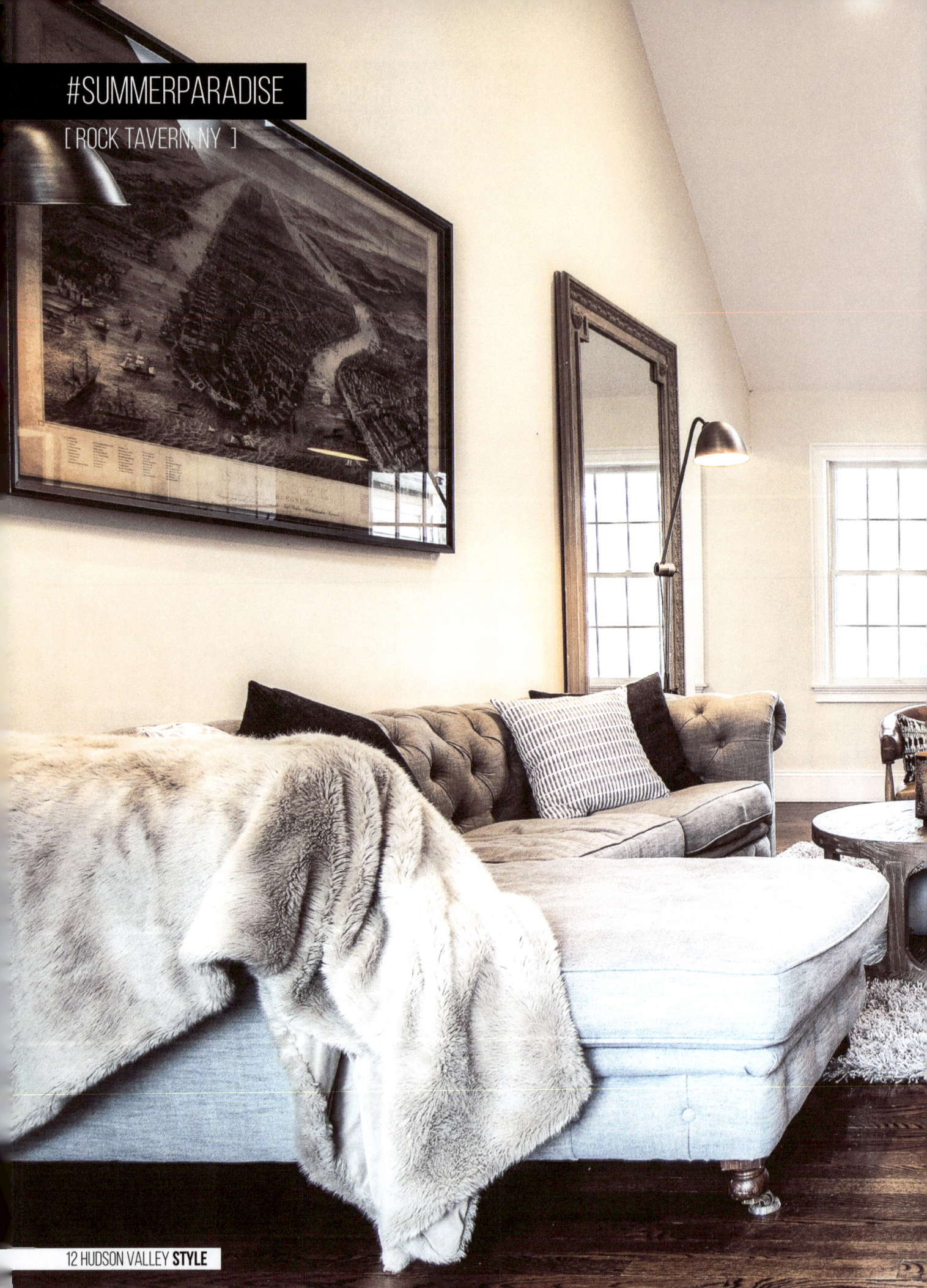
#SUMMERPARADISE
[ROCK TAVERN, NY]

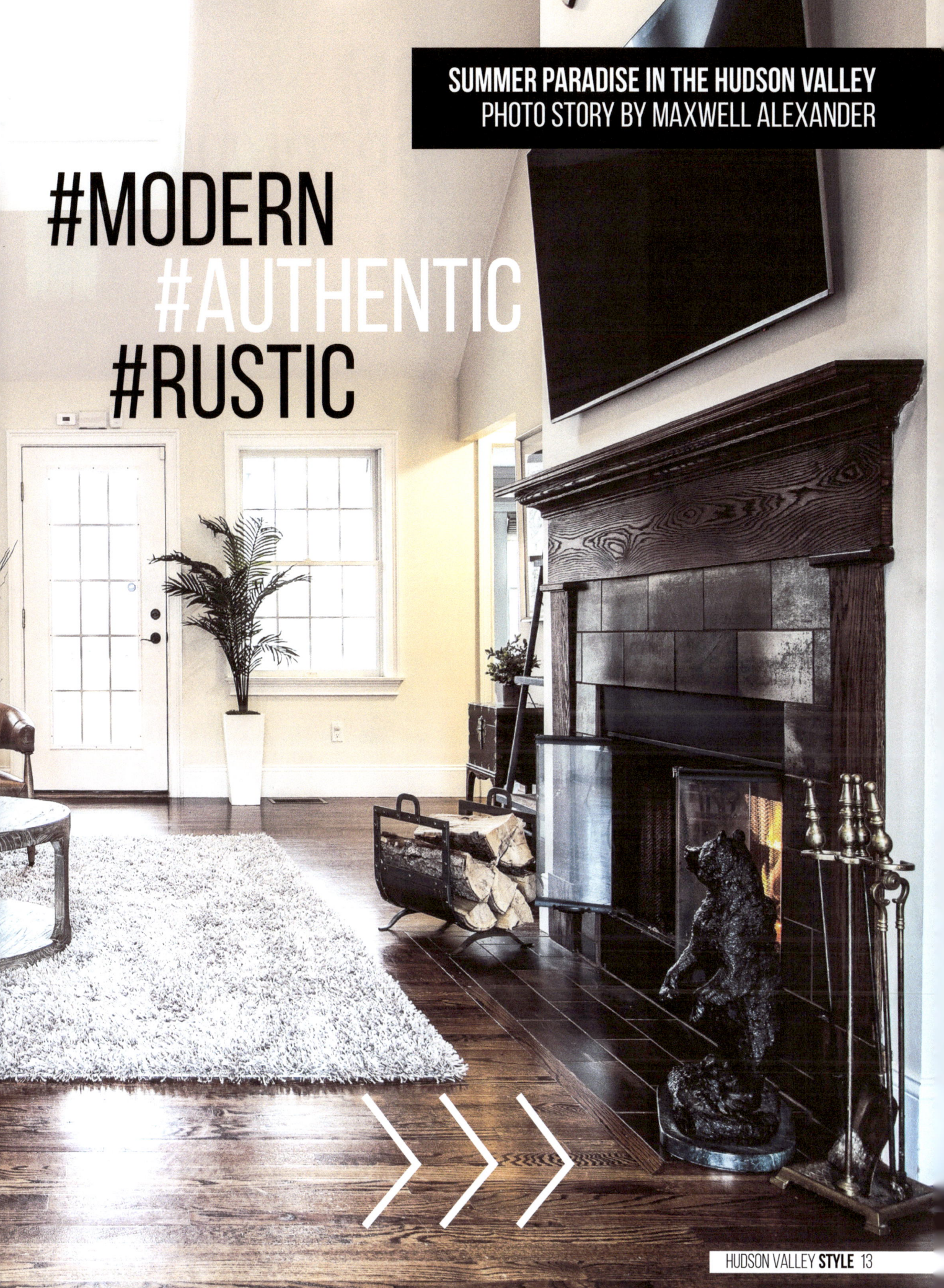

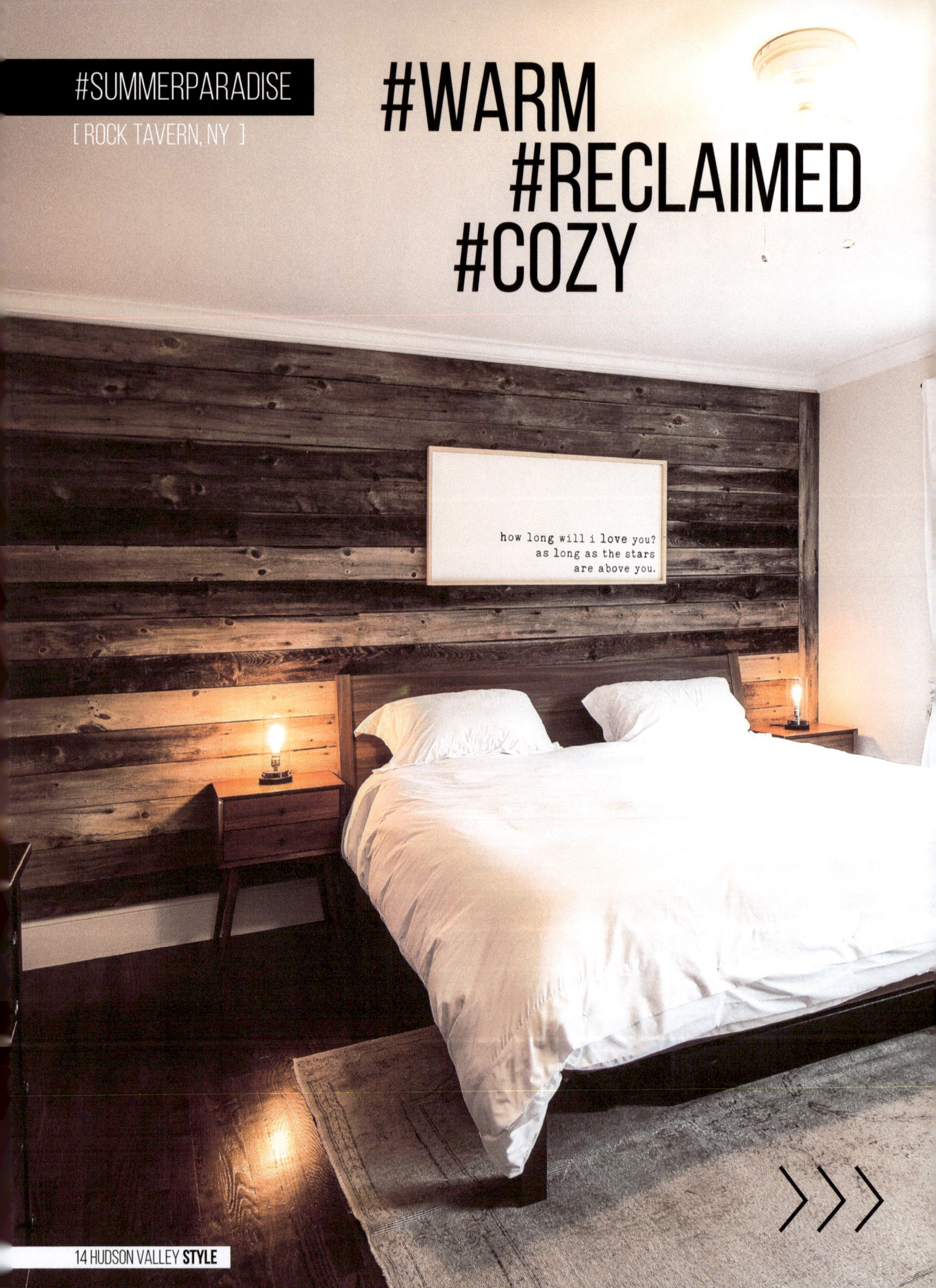

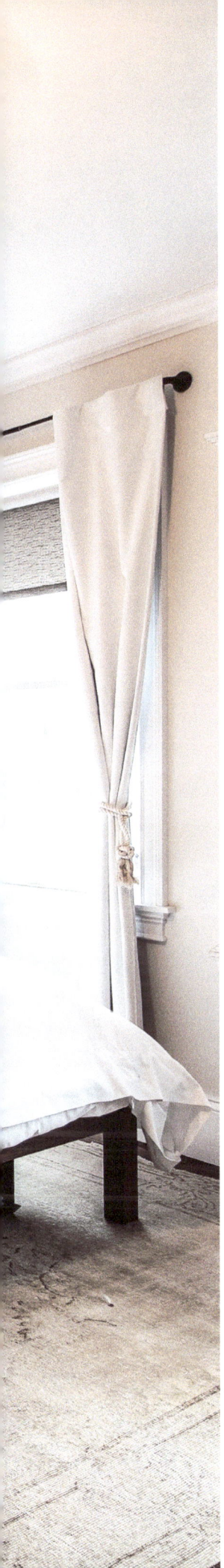

SUMMER PARADISE IN THE HUDSON VALLEY
PHOTO STORY BY MAXWELL ALEXANDER

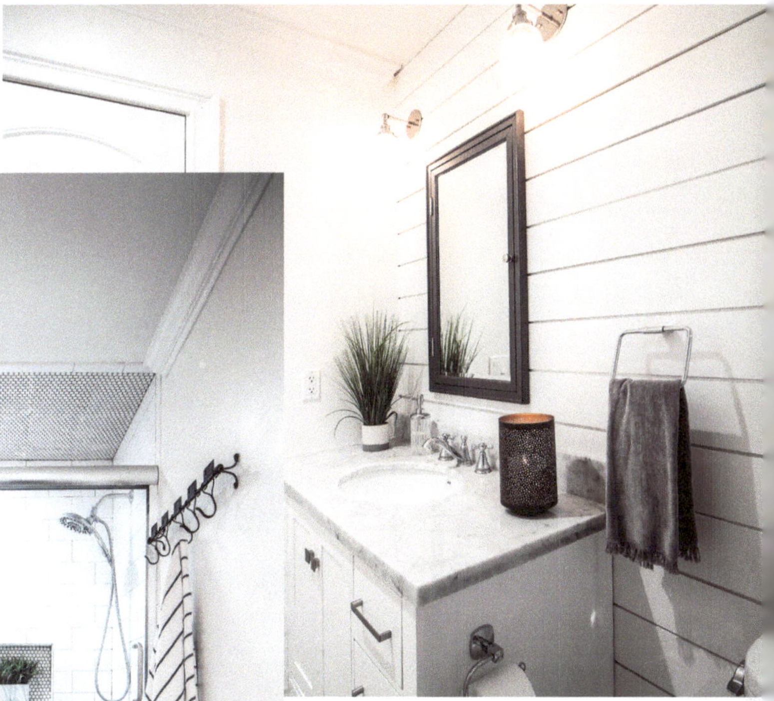

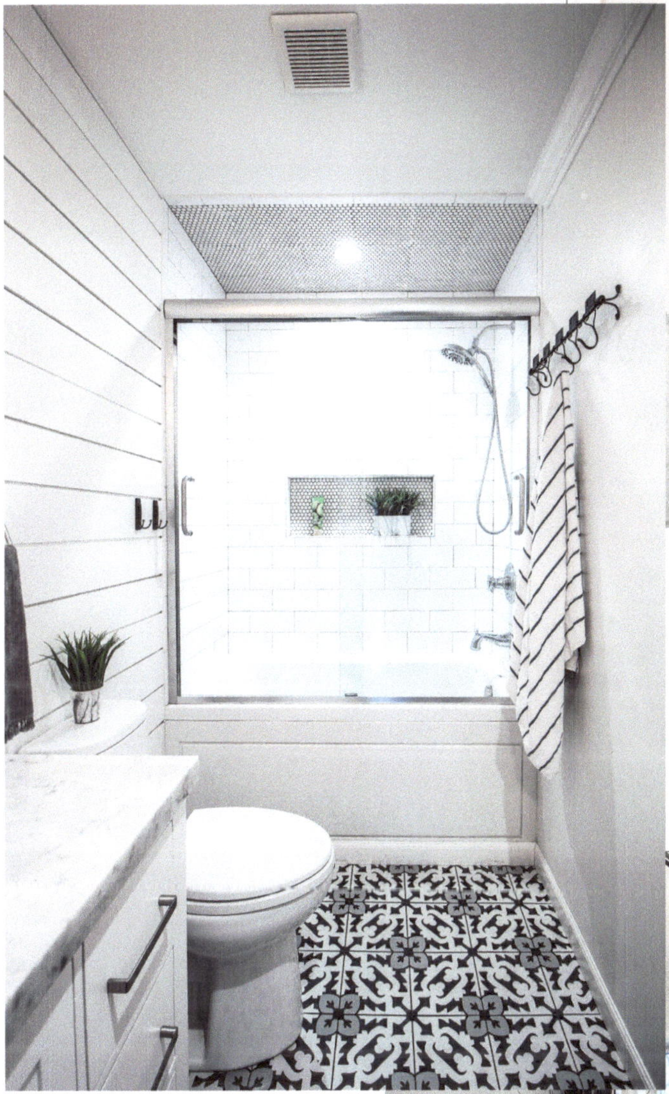

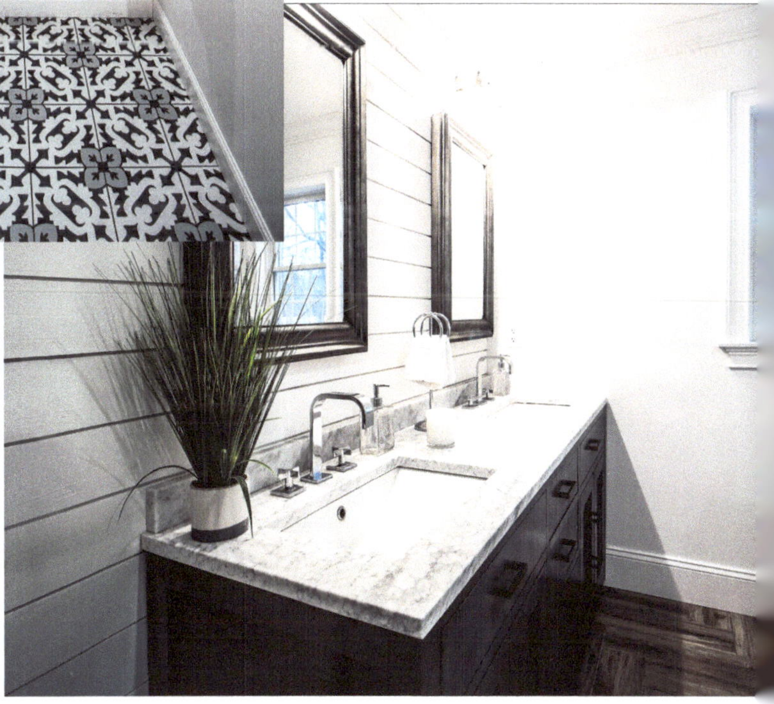

>>>

#WHITE
#CLEAN
#SHIPLAP

HUDSON VALLEY **STYLE** 15

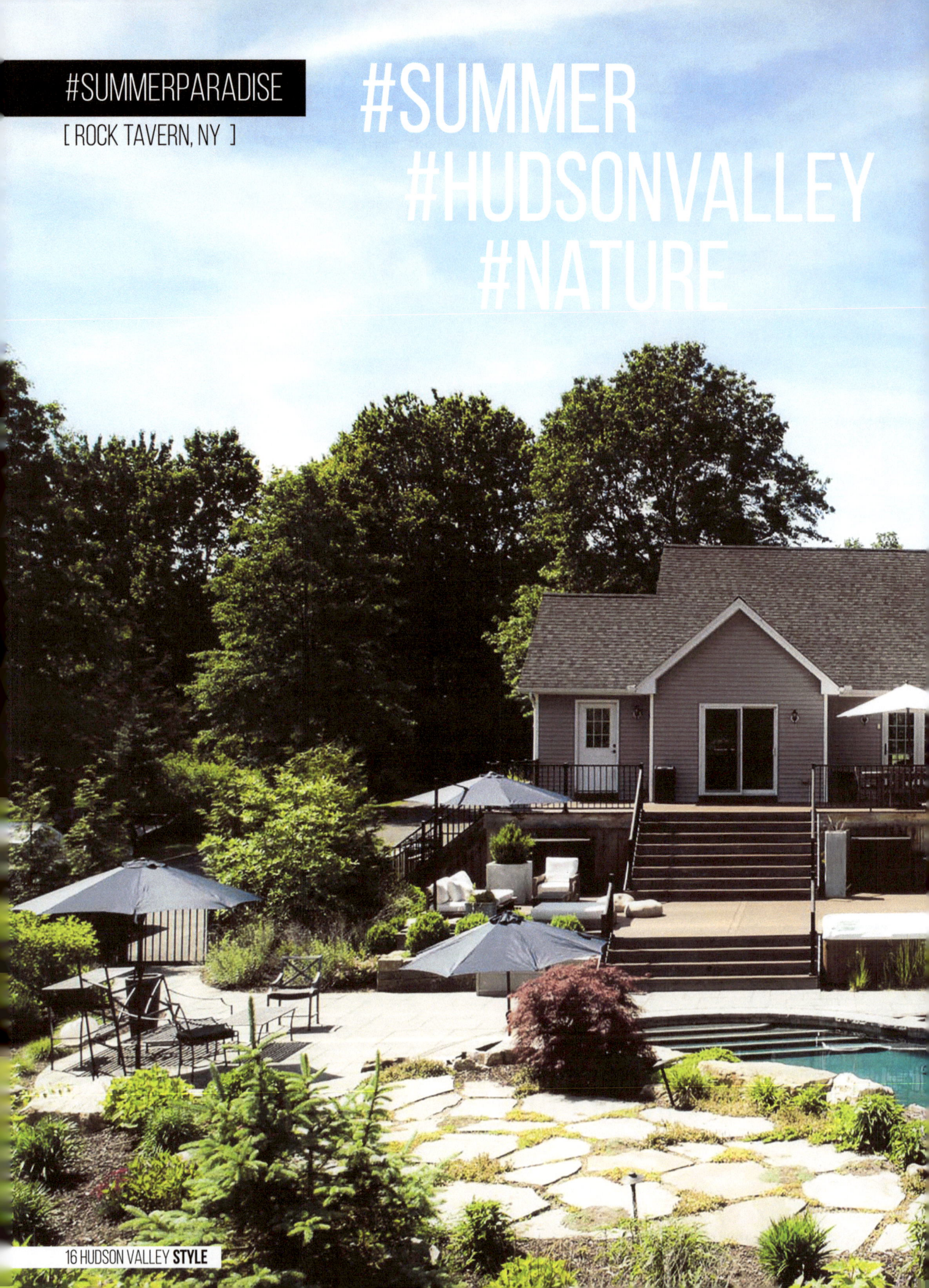

#SUMMERPARADISE
[ROCK TAVERN, NY]

#SUMMER
#HUDSONVALLEY
#NATURE

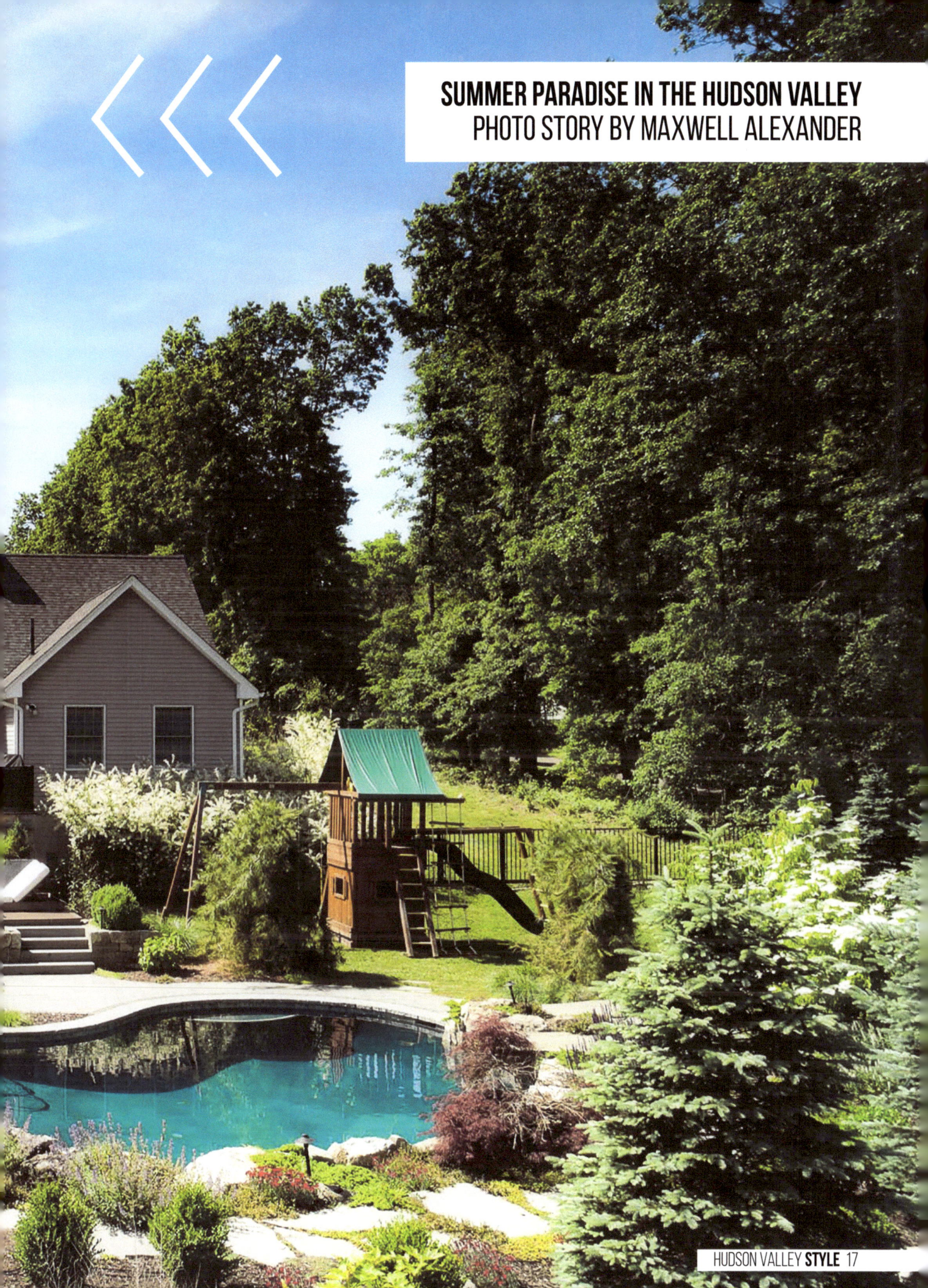

SUMMER PARADISE IN THE HUDSON VALLEY
PHOTO STORY BY MAXWELL ALEXANDER

#FARMHOUSEREINVENTED

[MARLBORO, NY]

A HISTORIC HUDSON VALLEY FARMHOUSE REINVENTED

STORY & PHOTOGRAPHY
BY **MAXWELL ALEXANDER**

Welcome to the historic (circa 1870) Hudson Valley Farmhouse in the heart of legendary Marlboro, NY. It has been completely reimagined by the Award-Winning Duncan Avenue Design Studio and has become an inspiring, stylish and extremely comfortable zero-emissions 21st century smart home just minutes away from NYC. Situated on top of a hill and an acre of picturesque landscape, it could become your turnkey second-home, a vacation home, rental or investment property, or an authentic Hudson Valley Style dream home for generations to come.

The Farmhouse has been renovated with style, design, sustainability, functionality, and comfort in mind and incorporates more than a dozen smart technology, energy efficiency, and sustainability features.

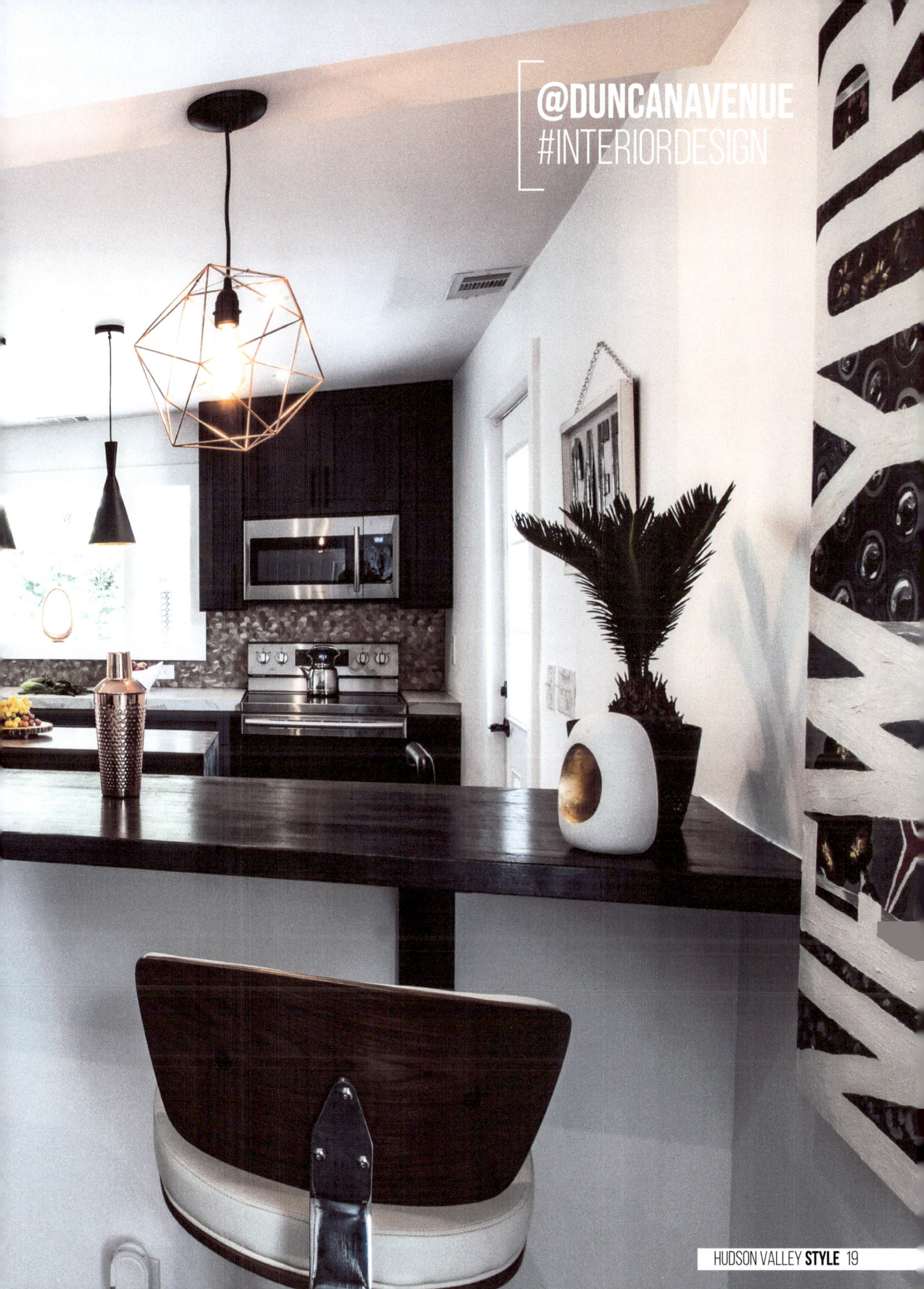

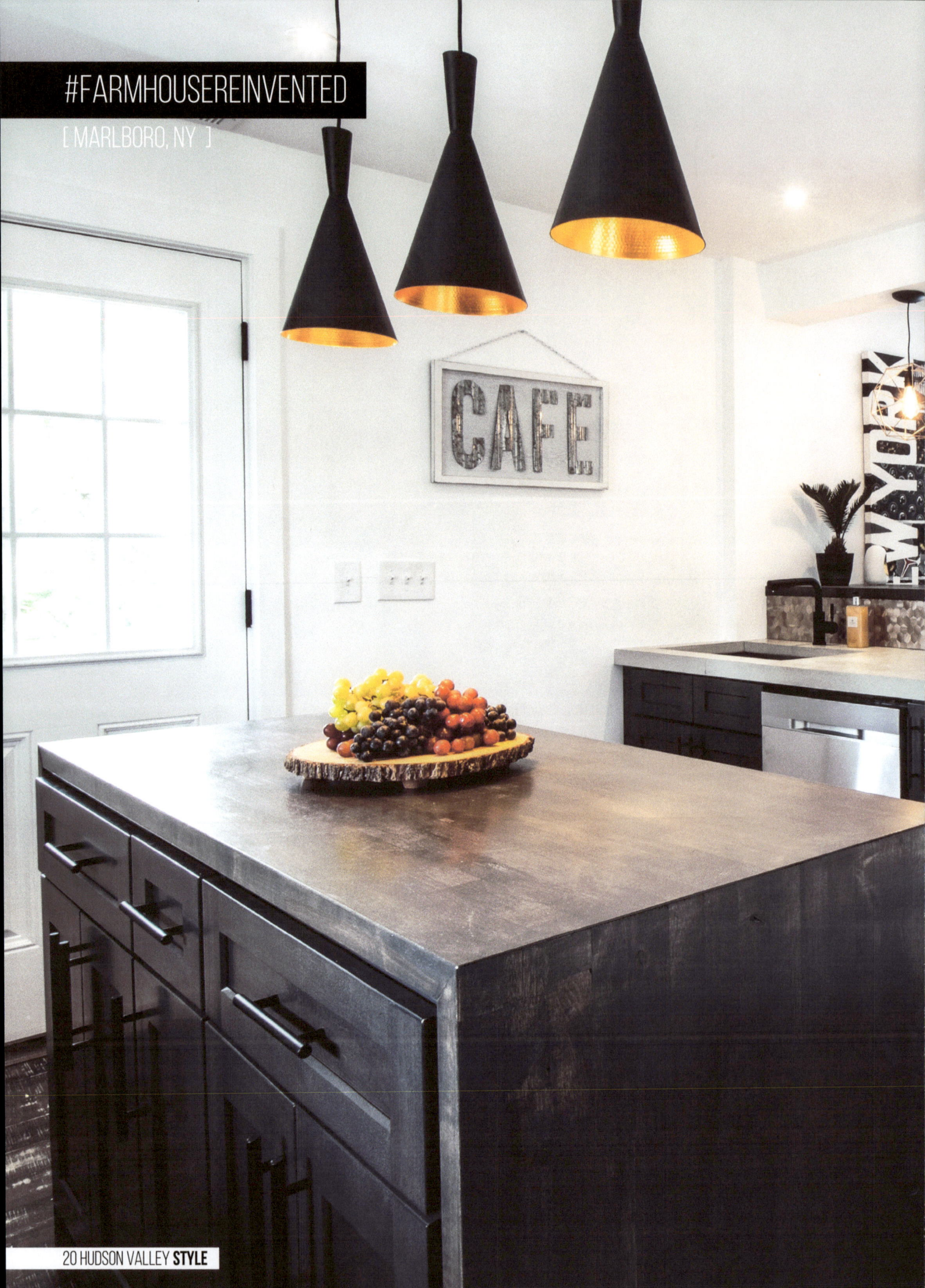

Contemporary open concept floorplan, glass french doors and 210° wraparound porch with 3-season outdoor dining space blur the line between indoor and outdoor living and allow residents and guests to enjoy a true connection with surrounding nature.

Wake up to the sunrise shining through double glass doors on the east side of the house and watch the warm sunset rays shining through plenty of energy-efficient windows and french doors on the west. High-end finishes such as sustainable bamboo hardwood floors, sustainable concrete countertops, solid wood kitchen cabinets with soft closing drawers, energy star stainless steel appliances, and designer light fixtures are only a few of the updates along with a brand-new central HVAC heat pump system controlled by smart Nest thermostat with two-zone sensors.

CONTEMPORARY SMART FLOOR PLAN

Brand new roof, utilities, and all LED lighting bring additional value and comfort for many years to come. The property features a beautiful designer pergola on the edge of the hill with an opportunity for the in-ground infinity pool. Property's sun number is 91 and is all set for installation of your own solar farm that will take the property go 100% off-grid.

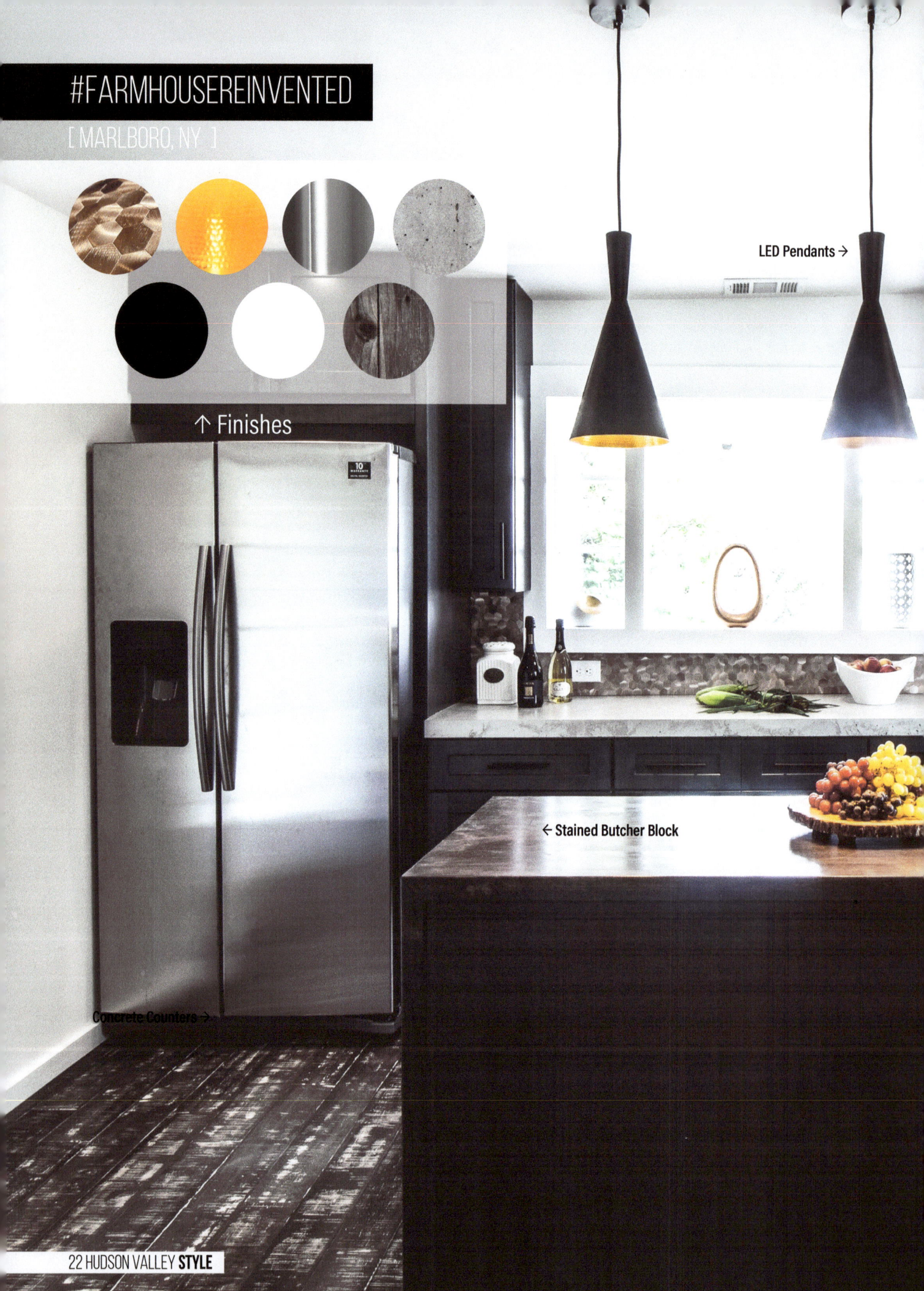

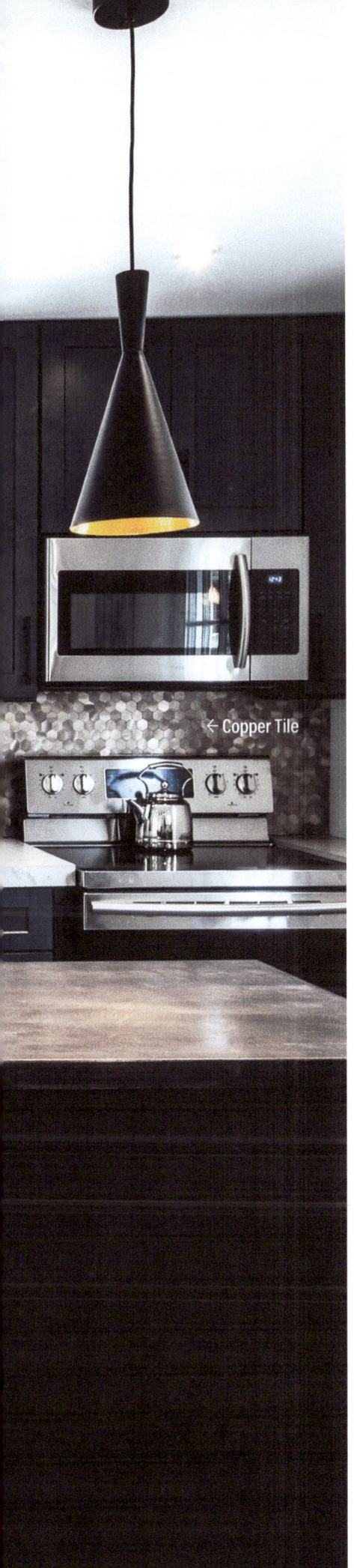

← Copper Tile

SUSTAINABLE CONCRETE & WOOD COUNTERTOPS

This kitchen has a lot of character thanks to the sophisticated/industrial look of concrete countertops. They are not just trendy, but also environmentally-friendly. One of the unique characteristics of concrete is that this material will evolve and adopt character over time, so the appearance of your counters will improve with age. Concrete counters are durable and heat-resistant for all of you avid bakers out there. The material is non-toxic, does not emit VOCs unlike plastics/polymers and is a sustainable material, unlike granite or marble. Concrete is a friend of the environment in all stages of its life span, from raw material production to demolition, making it a natural choice for sustainable home construction.

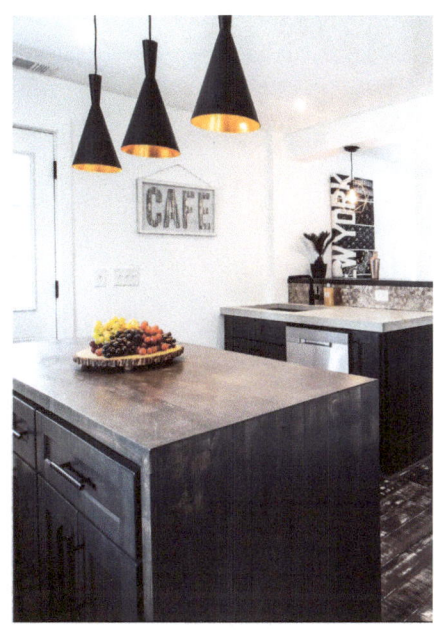

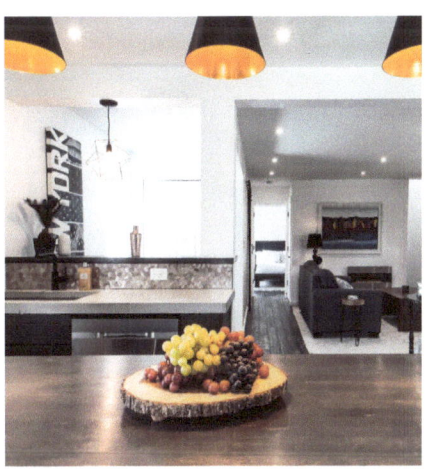

STAINLESS STEEL ENERGY STAR APPLIANCES

Stainless Steel Energy Star Appliances are an important accord in an overall symphony of this amazing and functional kitchen. They are positioned in the most efficient way to ensure an easy cooking process. The kitchen features range hood vented outside of the house and stylish yet environmentally-friendly electric range. Hudson Valley region energy providers offer an option to switch to 100% renewable electricity from wind and solar, so the electric range makes a lot of sense.

HUDSON VALLEY **STYLE** 23

#FARMHOUSEREINVENTED
[MARLBORO, NY]

NATURAL PATTERNS CERAMIC TILE MATTE BLACK ACCENTS

Natural look and natural materials. This time we went with darker accents colors, but overall both bathrooms in this house are bright and airy.

FLOATING VANITIES & BARN DOORS, CERAMIC TILE, DESIGNER LED LIGHT FIXTURES, AN ABUNDANCE OF LIGHT & SPACE CREATE AN INSPIRING SPA-LIKE EXPERIENCE

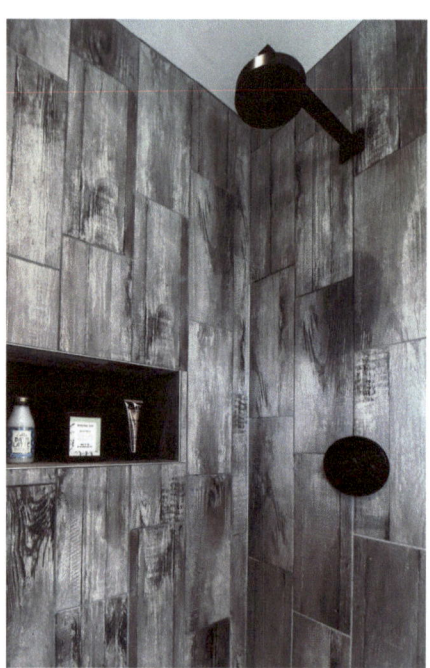

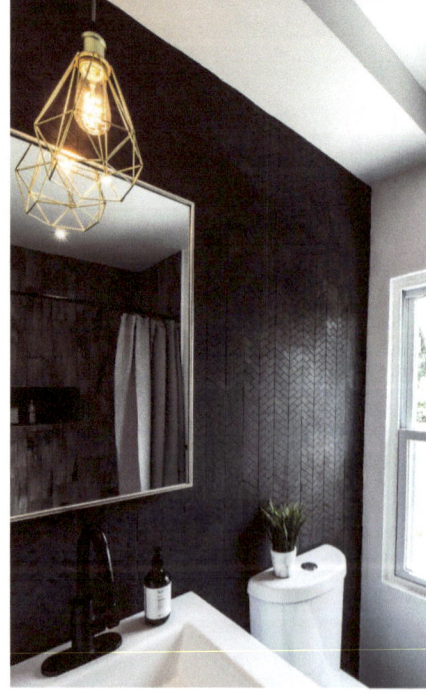

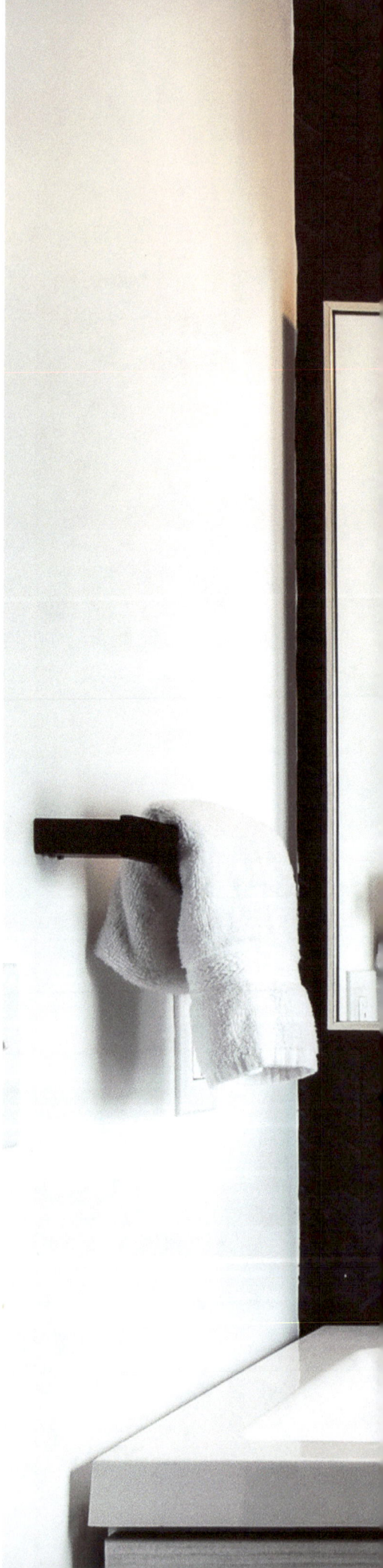

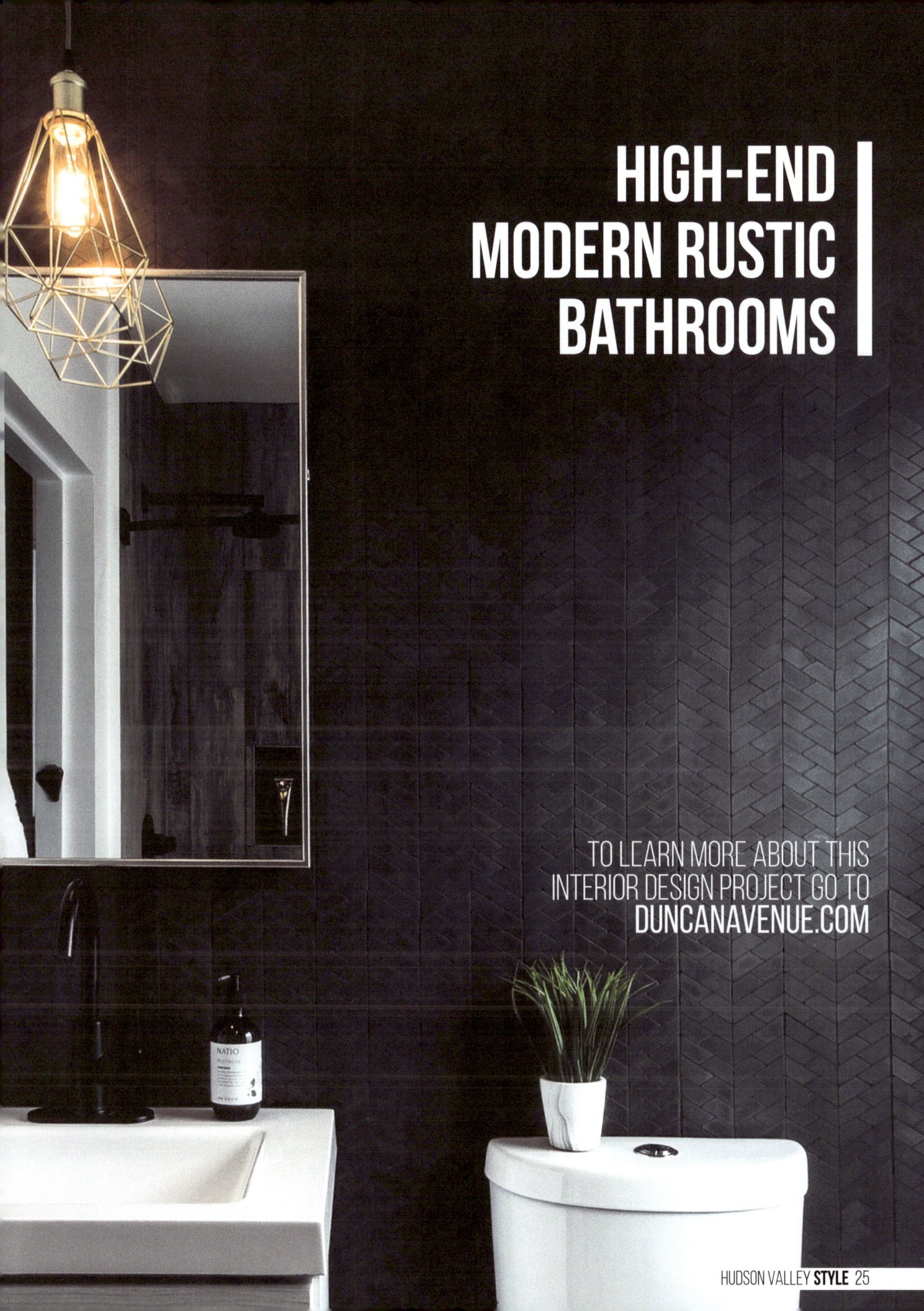

HIGH-END MODERN RUSTIC BATHROOMS

TO LEARN MORE ABOUT THIS INTERIOR DESIGN PROJECT GO TO
DUNCANAVENUE.COM

#SPRINGFASHION COVER STORY
[PHOENICIA, NY]

SPRING FASHION PHOTO STORY BY HELENA PALZZI

Contributing Photo Editor/Photographer and Art Direction:
Helena Palazzi
helenapalazzi.com

Model:
Viktoria Viktorenkova
@ Supreme Models, NY

Wardrobe/Styling:
Leah Levin
leahlevin.com

Hair:
Hikari Tezuka
@art department, NY

Makeup:
Marie-Josèe Leduc
@art department, NY

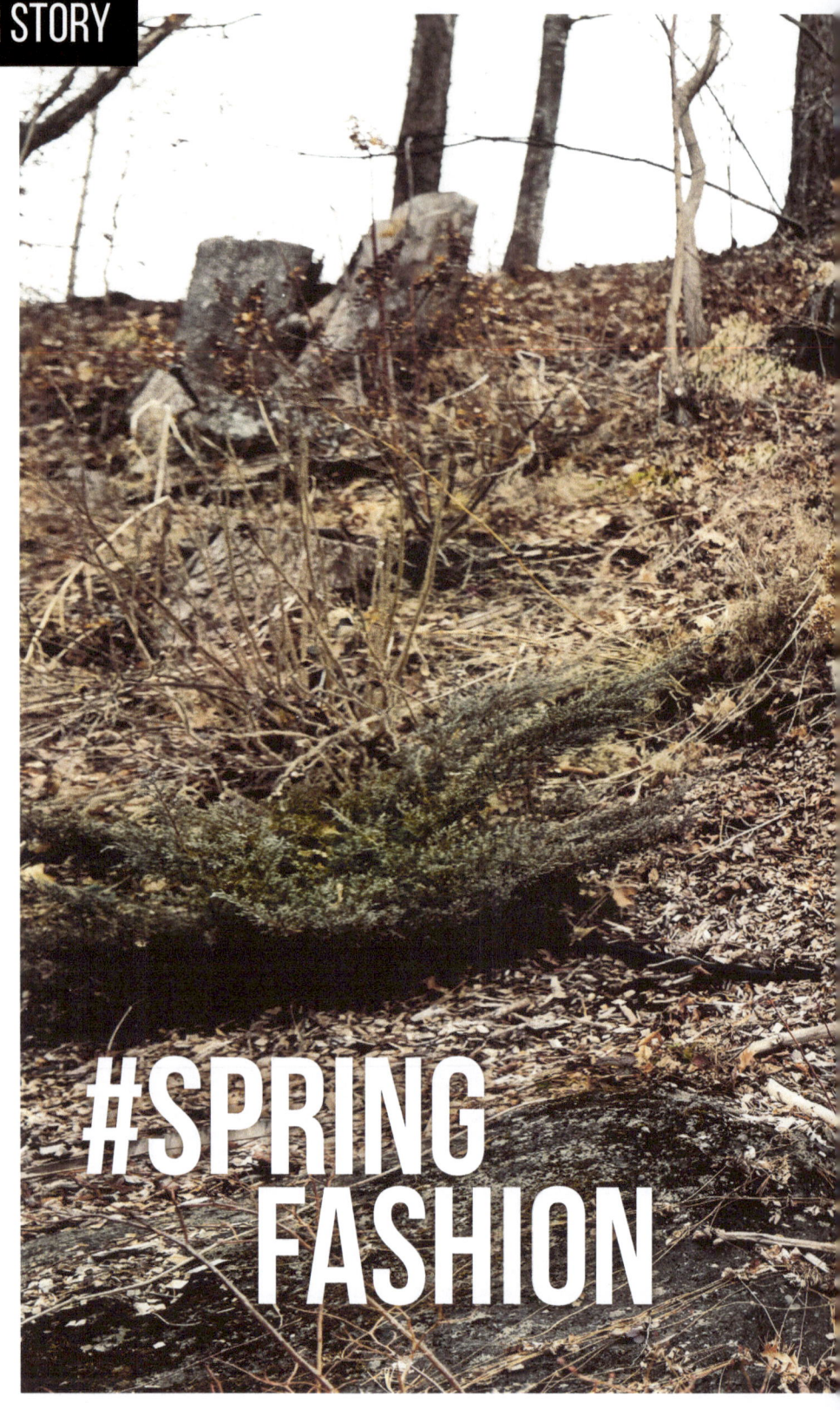

#SPRING FASHION

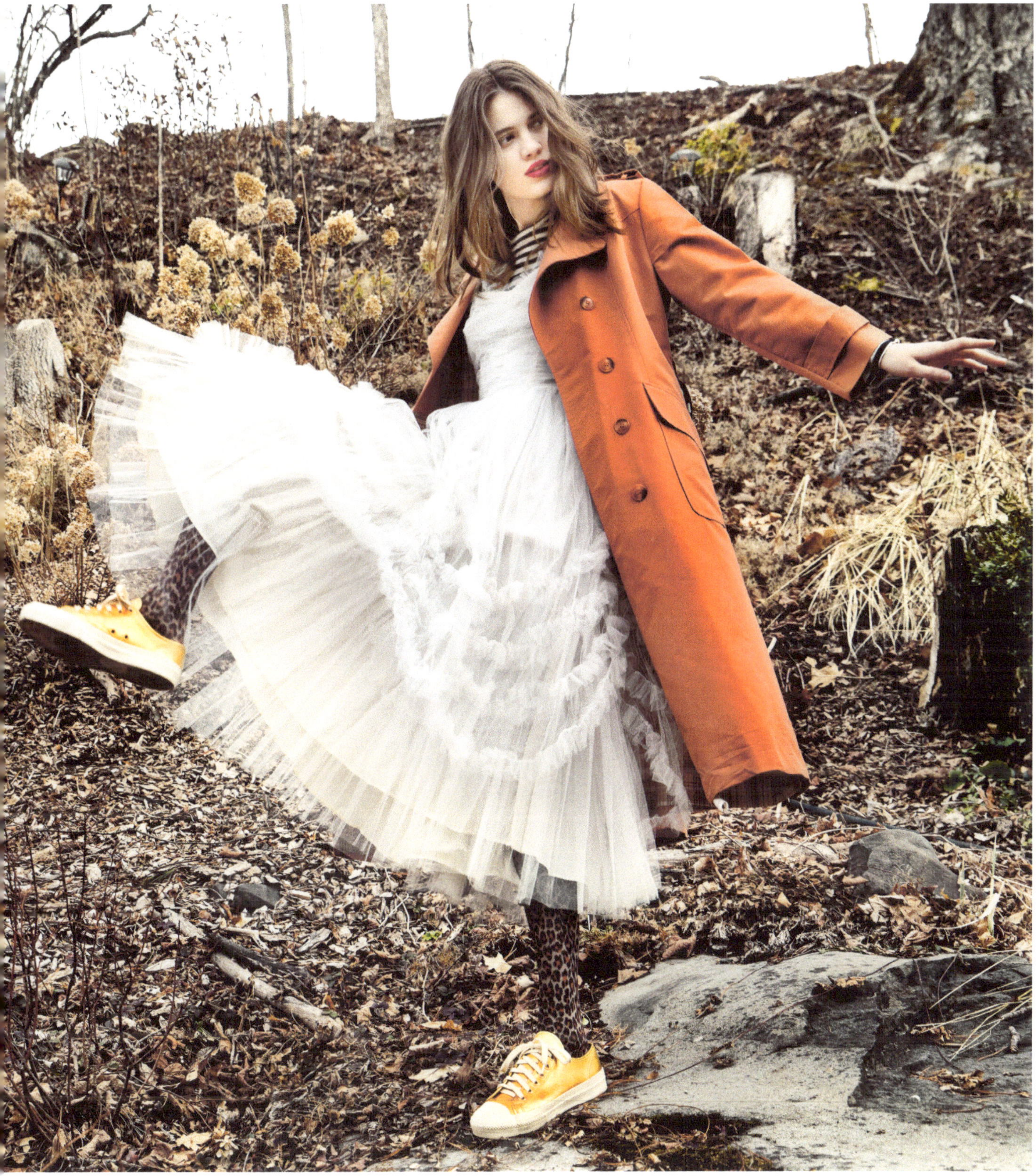

Coat and Dress: Lovefield Vintage
Tights: HUE
Sneakers: Stylist Own

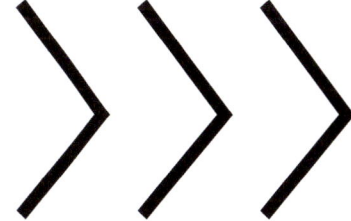

#SPRINGFASHION COVER STORY

[PHOENICIA, NY]

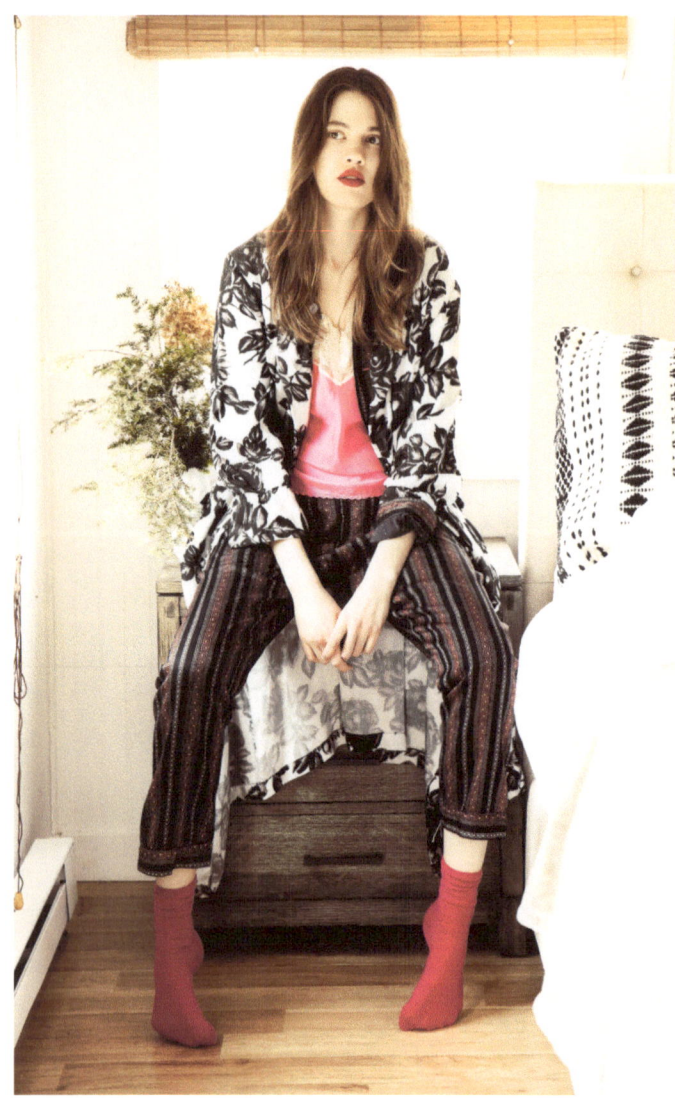

Vintage robe, pajamas and camisole @leahlevin
Socks: HUE

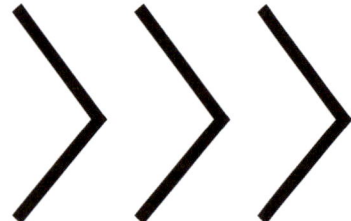

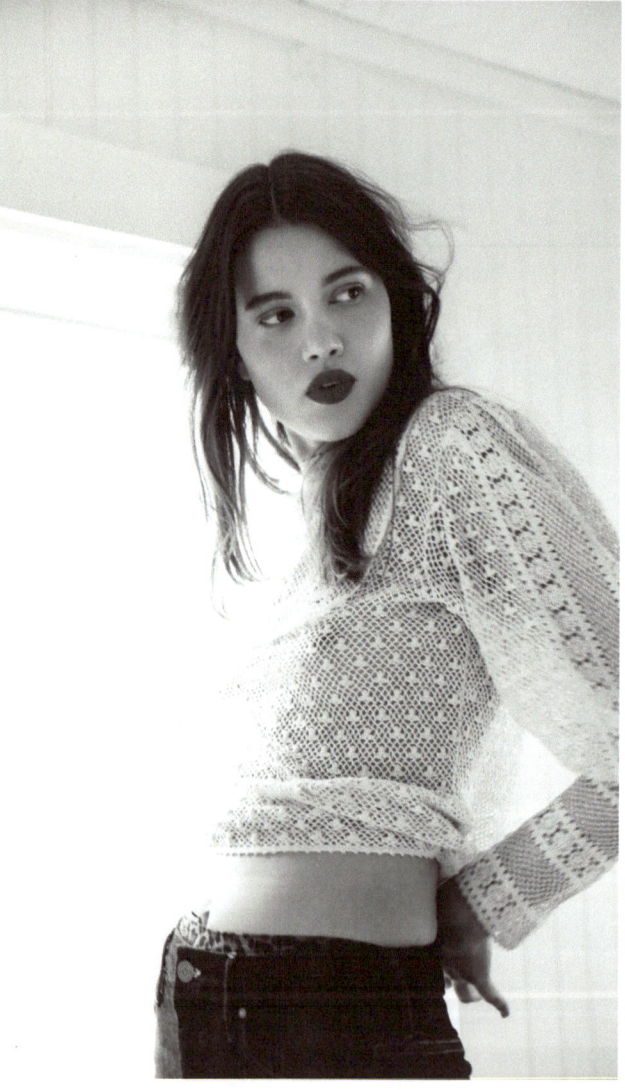

Vintage crochet top @leahlevin
Jeans: Next Boutique
Tights: HUE

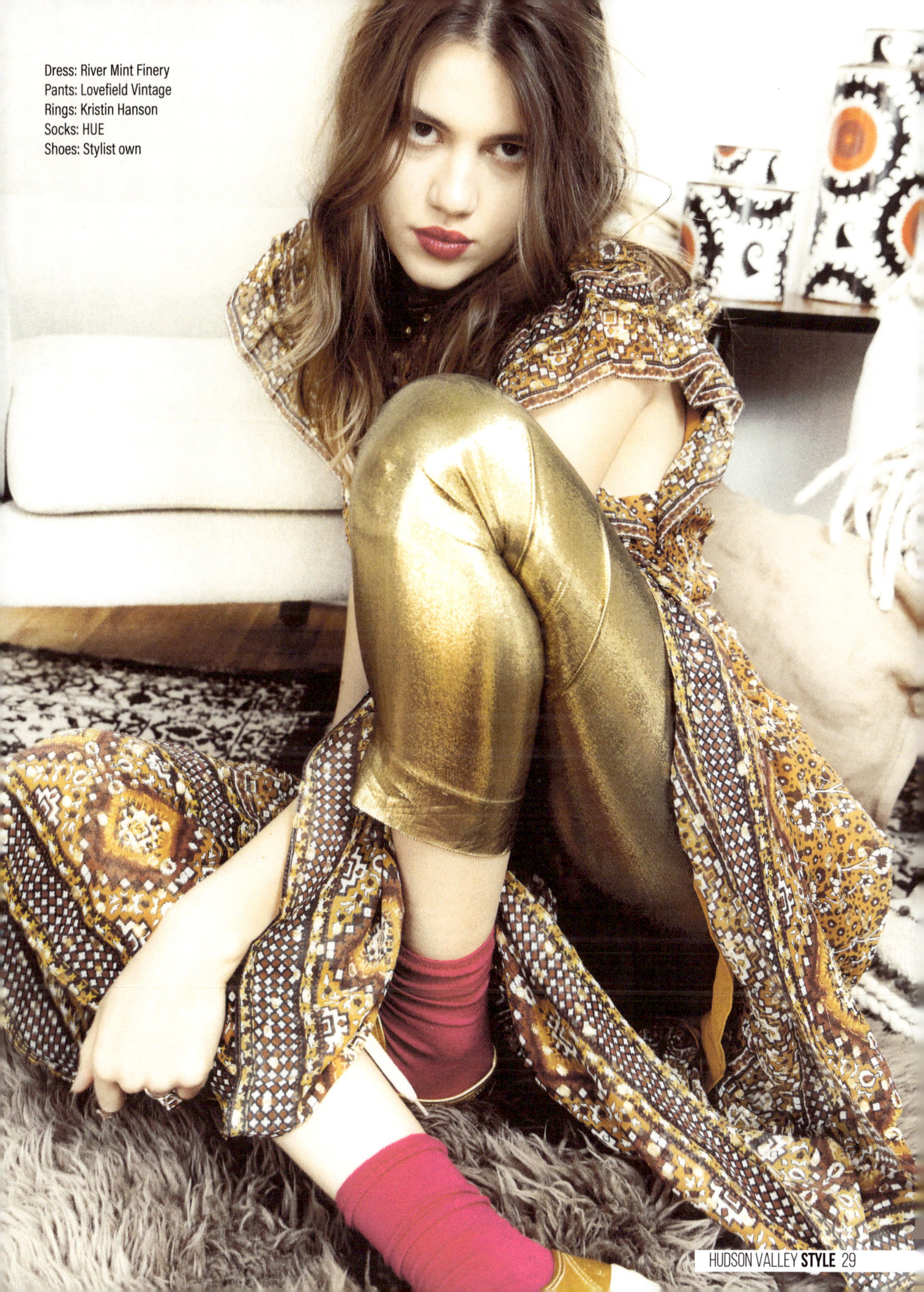

Dress: River Mint Finery
Pants: Lovefield Vintage
Rings: Kristin Hanson
Socks: HUE
Shoes: Stylist own

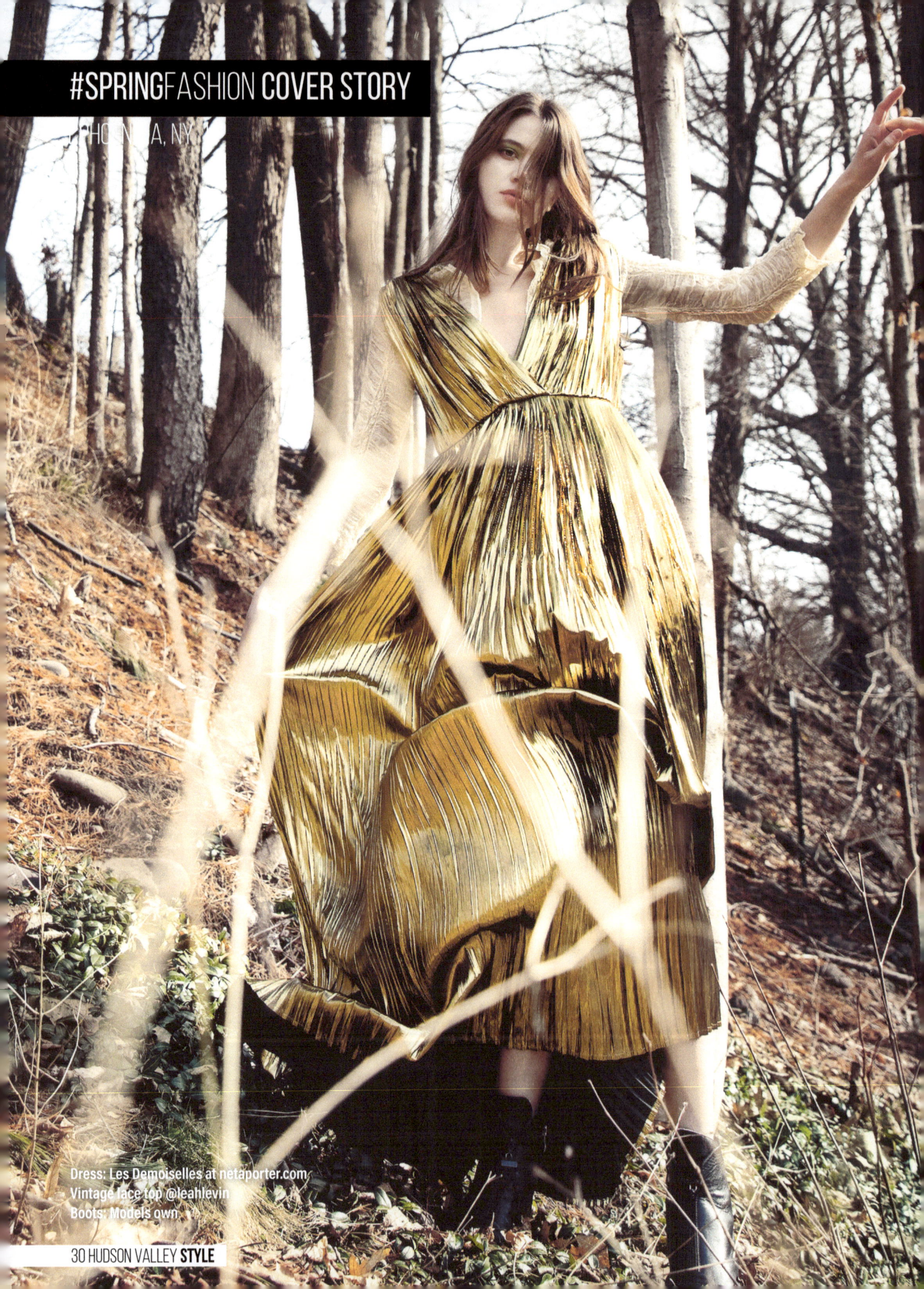

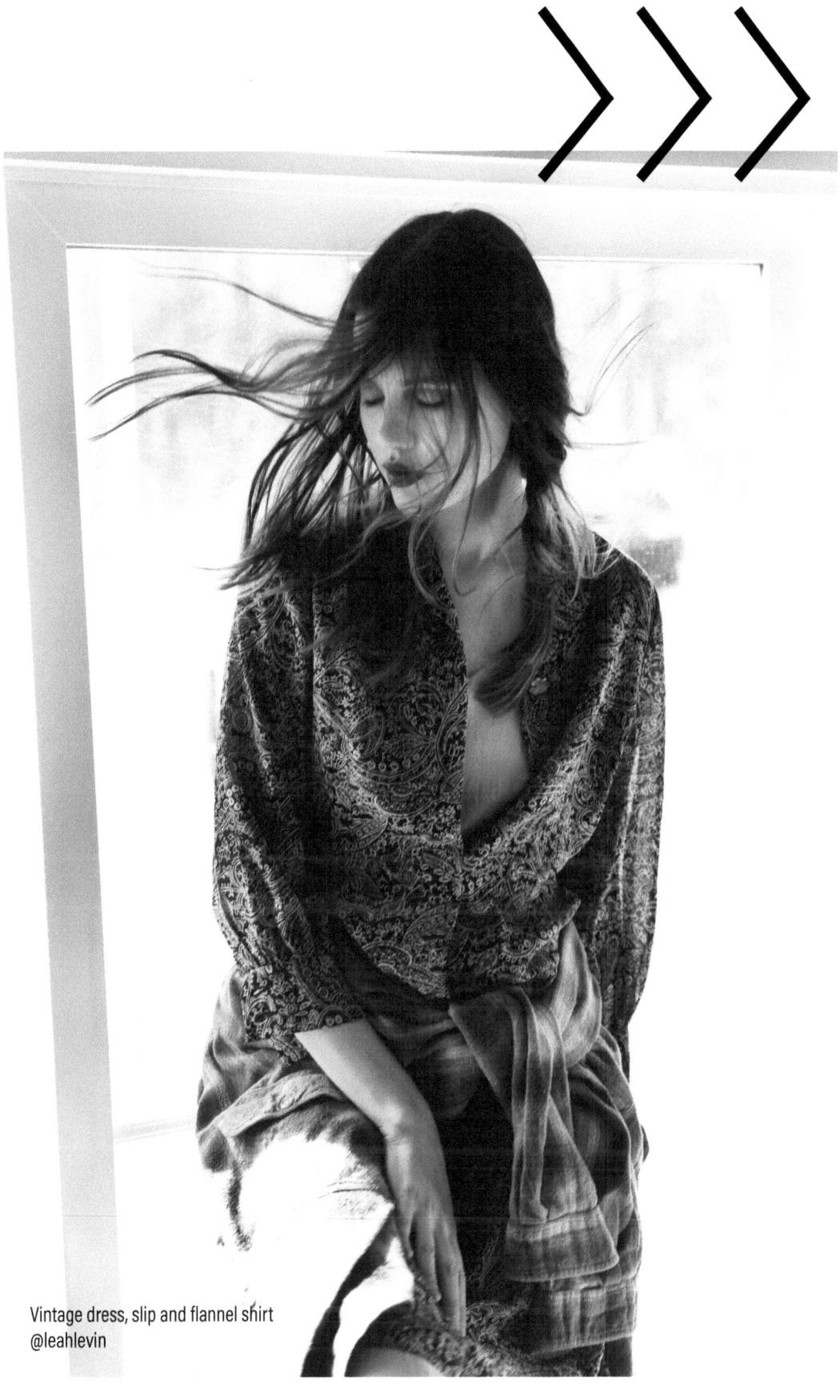

Vintage dress, slip and flannel shirt
@leahlevin

#SPRINGFASHION COVER STORY
[PHOENICIA, NY]

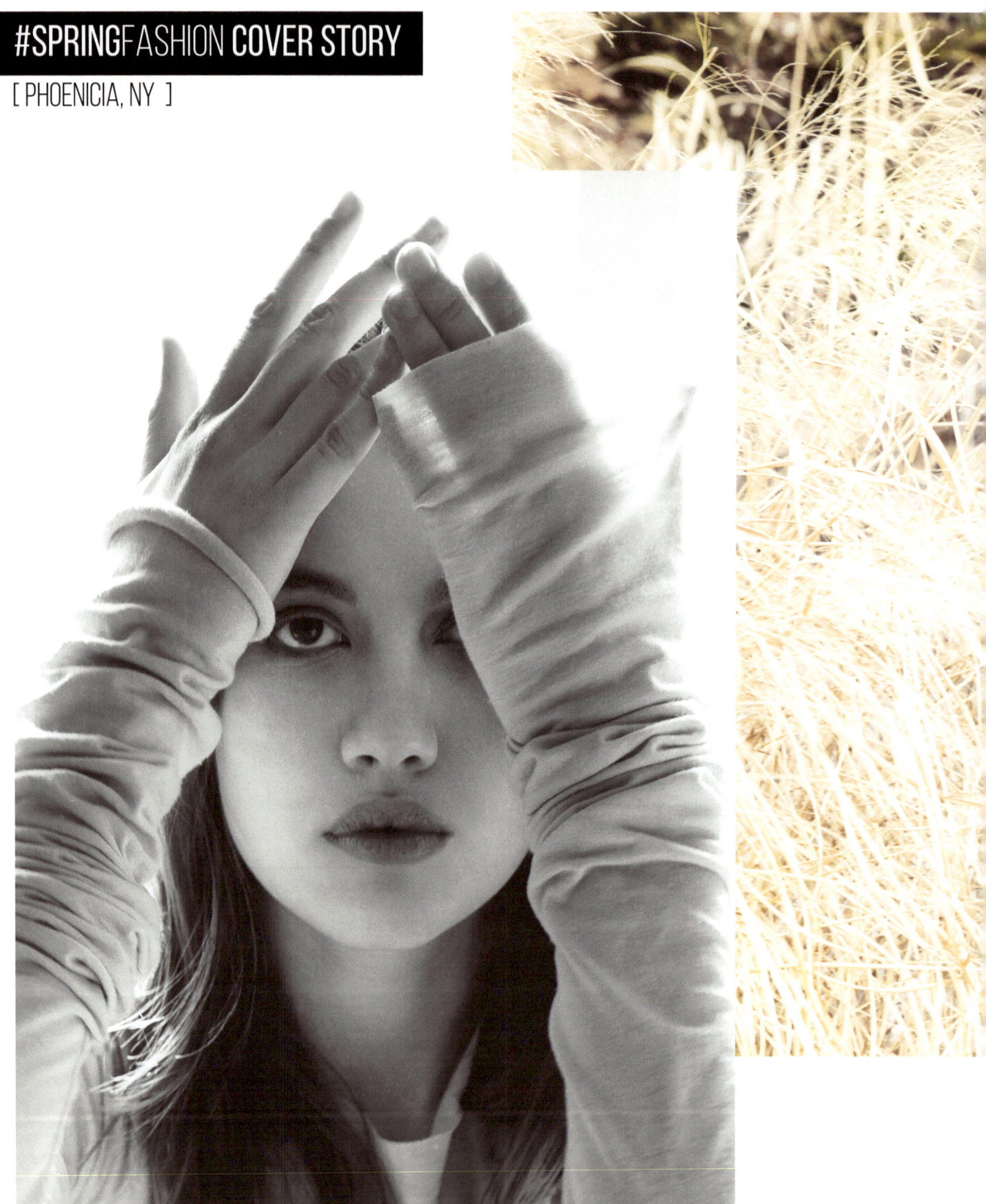

Long sleeve top: Zephyr
Earrings: River Mint Finery

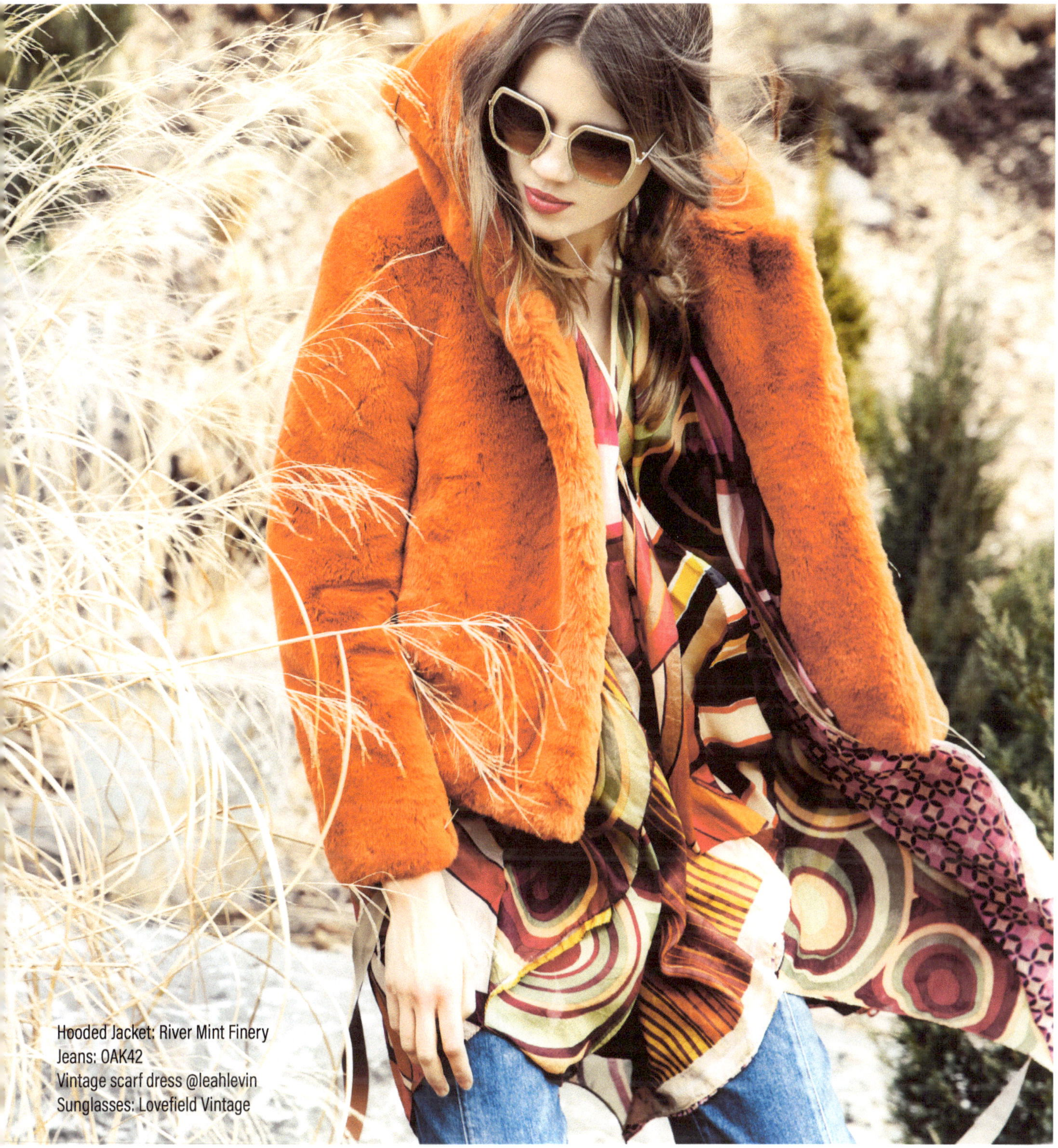

Hooded Jacket: River Mint Finery
Jeans: OAK42
Vintage scarf dress @leahlevin
Sunglasses: Lovefield Vintage

Contributing clothing and design stores in Kingston:
River Mind Finery https://www.rivermintfinery.com/
Oak42 https://www.oak42.com/
Lovefield Vintage https://www.lovefieldvintage.com/
Next Boutique http://nextboutique.com/
Zephyr on Hudson https://zephyr-on-hudson.com/
Kristin Hanson Jewelry https://www.kristinhanson.us/

Photoshoot Location designed by AHG: https://arthomegarden.com/
If you would like to be featured in upcoming issues please reach out to us!

WHO IS YOUR BUYER?

[MILLENNIALS]

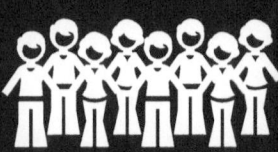

36%
[THE LARGEST MARKET SHARE]

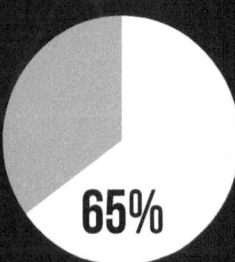
65%
FIRST-TIME HOME BUYERS

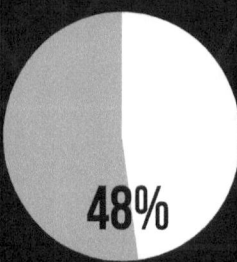
48%
HAVE CHILDREN

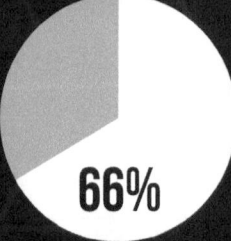
66%
MARRIED COUPLES

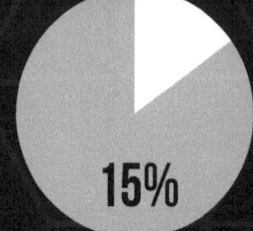
15%
UNMARRIED COUPLES

GENERATION X 38-52 Y/O

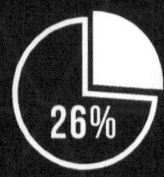
26%
[OF ALL HOMEBUYERS]

$104,700
[MEDIAN INCOME]

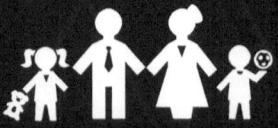
MOST LIKELY TO BE MARRIED & MOST LIKELY TO HAVE CHILDREN

MOST RACIALLY & ETHNICALLY DIVERSE
26%
IDENTIFYING THEY ARE A RACE **OTHER THAN** WHITE/CAUCASIAN

 BUY THE LARGEST HOMES IN MEDIAN SQFT.

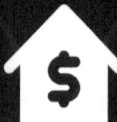 PURCHASE THE HIGHEST MEDIAN PRICED HOMES

[YOUNGER BABY BOOMERS]
53-62 Y/O
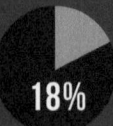 **18%**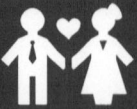

[OLDER BABY BOOMERS]
63-71 Y/O
14%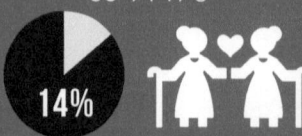

[THE SILENT GENERATION]
72-92 Y/O
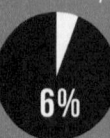 **6%**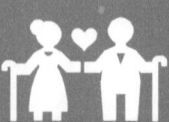

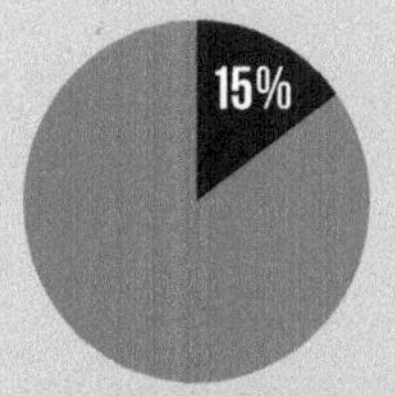

15%
15% OF ALL BUYERS PURCHASED NEW CONSTRUCTION

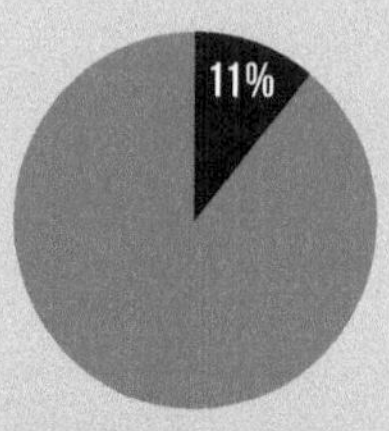

11%
11% OF MILLENNIALS PURCHASED NEW CONSTRUCTION

85% PURCHASED PREVIOUSLY OWNED HOMES
[MILLENNIALS: 89%]

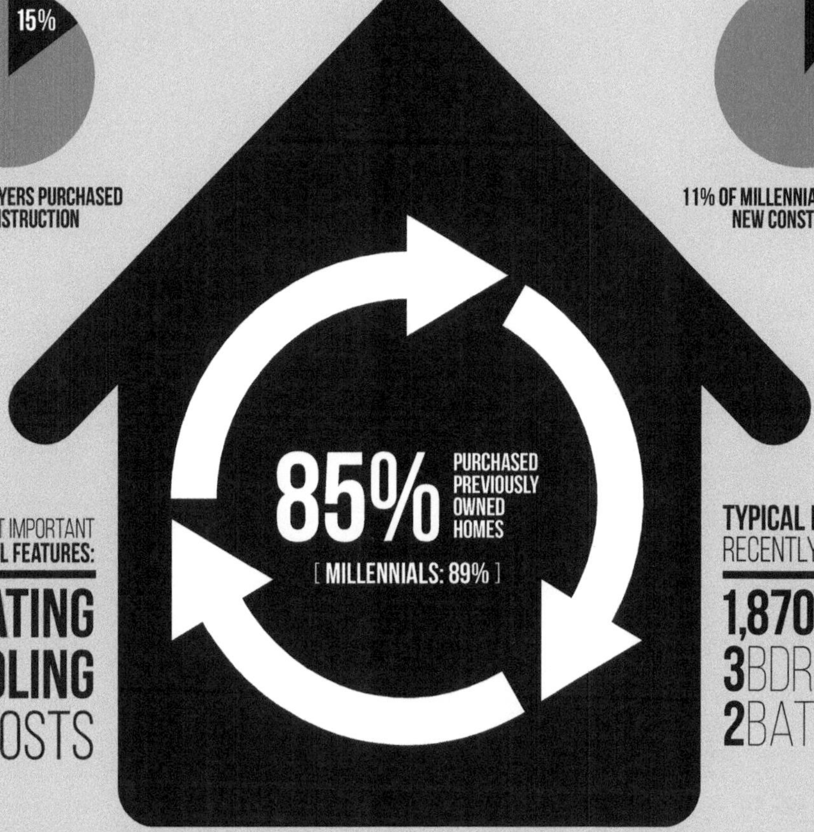

MOST IMPORTANT ENVIRONMENTAL FEATURES:
HEATING & COOLING COSTS

TYPICAL HOME RECENTLY PURCHASED
1,870 SQFT.
3 BDRM.
2 BATH.

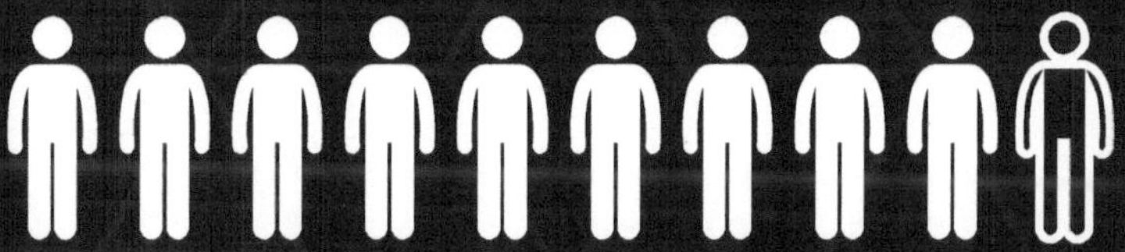

90%

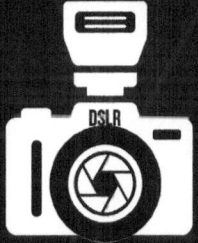

"90% OF BUYERS UNDER AGE OF 62 CONSIDER PHOTOGRAPHY AS THE MOST IMPORTANT FEATURE WHEN SEARCHING ONLINE"

DATA SOURCE: 2018 HOME BUYER AND SELLER GENERATIONAL TRENDS REPORT BY THE NATIONAL ASSOCIATION OF REALTORS®

almaxrealty ™
[ALEXANDER MAXWELL REALTY]

SELLING YOUR PROPERTY?
ASK US ABOUT **COMPLIMENTARY** ALL-INCLUSIVE
STRATEGIC MARKETING PACKAGE

LOG ON TO **ALMAXREALTY.COM** & JOIN US ON INSTAGRAM! **@ALMAXREALTY**

[PRESENTED BY ALMAXREALTY.COM]

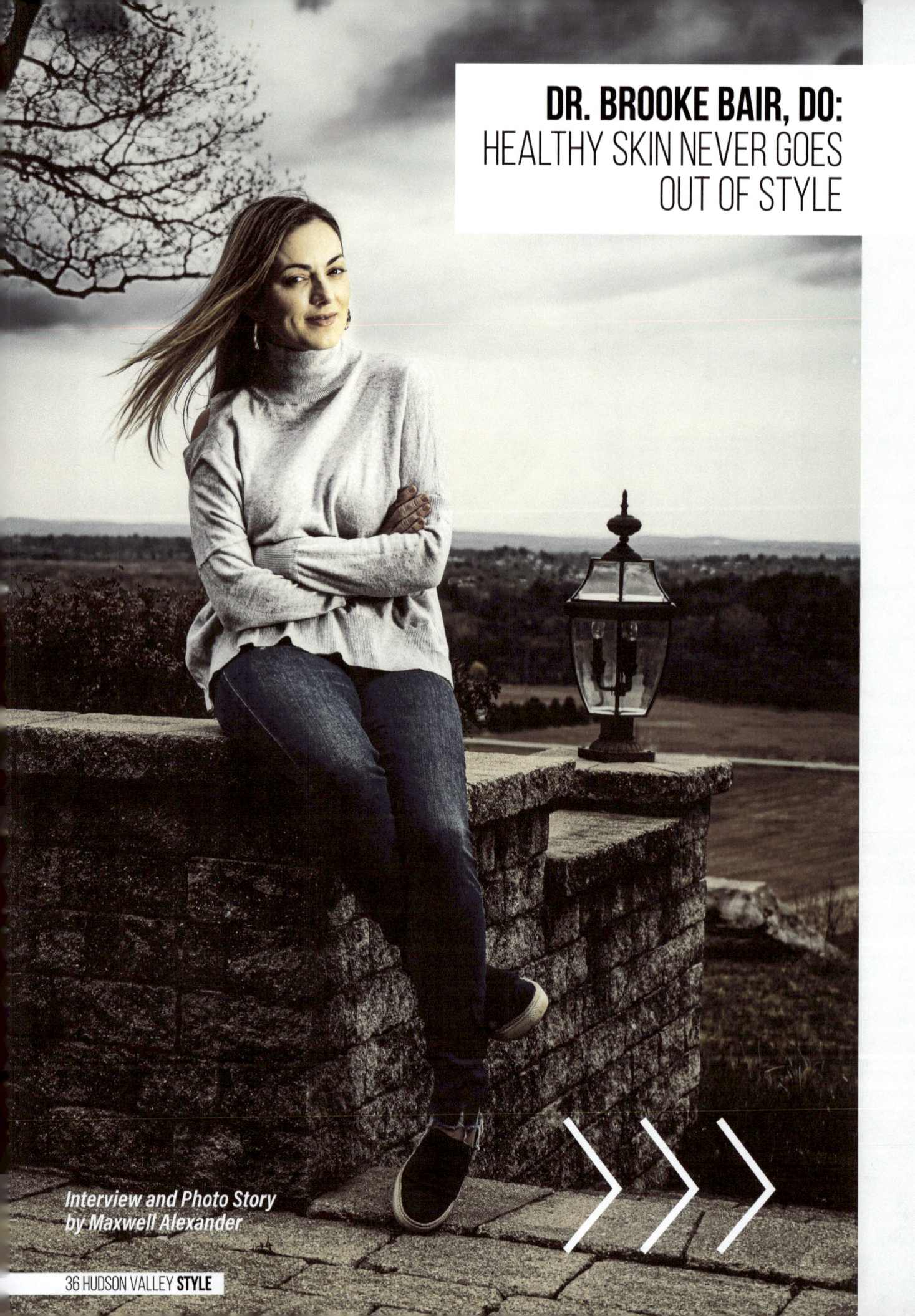

DR. BROOKE BAIR, DO:
HEALTHY SKIN NEVER GOES OUT OF STYLE

Interview and Photo Story by Maxwell Alexander

INTERVIEW WITH DR. BROOKE BAIR, DO

Dr. Bair, a Manhattan-based dermatologist, originally from Florida, has laid down roots in the Hudson Valley and expanded her dermatology practice to the area. She gives us the skinny on her favorite aesthetic procedures and how her new landscape has played a role.

"When I set out to start my dermatology practice in Manhattan, of course, I was scared. But, mostly, I was excited. After getting my city practice underway, I decided to open a part-time location in New Paltz, as we have family there. I found myself really drawn to the people and the atmosphere. Soon, I found that my family and I were spending more and more time upstate vs. the city."
- said Dr. Bair when I asked her how she made Hudson Valley her new home.

Before Dr. Brooke Bair, Do had opened her New Paltz office, Hudson Valley was lacking access to medical, surgical, and cosmetic dermatology from a board-certified dermatologist. Now it's here, and all services under one roof, including their new Kingston location.

Maxwell: When I saw your brand for the first time, I thought to myself "Here is another great example of someone knowing what they are doing right here in the Hudson Valley :)" But is there a story that is more than just great branding?

Dr. Bair: Starting my own business has been by far the most challenging thing I've ever done. As a mom, physician, and business owner, there is constant internal conflict about what or who in my life needs my attention. I feel guilty when I take a day off if there's a patient that needs me. I feel guilty for being at work instead of playing with my daughter. So there's this persistent mental gymnastics of "did I do my best for all the people in my life today?" Despite all these challenges, it has still been by far the most rewarding thing I've ever done. Undertaking such a special project, I had to give it a special name. This was actually becoming a problem because all the state and federal tax forms require a name, obviously. I couldn't move forward without one. "This naming exercise was WAY more challenging than picking a name for my daughter", I thought. And then there it was. My daughter was an infant when I started the process of opening the practice, and I couldn't think of anything more special than her. So I decided to name the practice Luna Dermatology after my daughter.

Maxwell: As a realtor, I've noticed quite a staggering migration of the millennial generation from New York City to the Hudson Valley. Are you a part of this phenomenon? And if so, why do you think this is happening now?

Dr. Bair: I suppose you could say that I am part of that movement. I think the Hudson Valley is a bit of a hidden gem. More and more people from the city are discovering that once they visit. Although, I will say I left New York City reluctantly, and at first, I felt pretty isolated. I missed my city patients. I missed my friends. I missed all the fun and exciting things to do in NYC. But, now, I couldn't be happier. It has

"I THINK THE HUDSON VALLEY IS A BIT OF A HIDDEN GEM."

been a great change for me and my family. We are closer to extended family now, too. With time, I had new patients and new friends. I just had to learn to be patient. In the city, you can get whatever you want, whenever you want. Up here, it just takes more time, but there are beauty and adventure in that discovery.

Maxwell: We define Hudson Valley Style as a blend of the metropolitan sophistication of New York City and the organic and rustic charm of the Hudson River Valley region. What is your take on that? Are you leaning more towards the concrete jungle or the flowery beginnings in your personal style? How did it change within the past year after you moved to the area?

Dr. Bair: In my field of dermatology and more specifically, aesthetic dermatology, I have to balance art with beauty and nature. This means offering bespoke treatment plans to maintain a natural, timeless, effortless look. Not overdone. I'm not trying to create the real housewives of Hudson Valley. Being down-to-earth, mindful, and practicing gratitude don't mean that we have to forego a bit of aesthetic pampering from time to time. It's best for me to try and get out in front of their concerns. It's possible to slow down the aging process...much harder to reverse it. So we encourage people to come in and start a gradual approach that will serve them better over the long term. I like to call it "tweakments" vs treatments – small gradual changes that are subtle, but effective. It's also nice that I can bring the latest, cutting-edge treatments from Manhattan to the Hudson Valley.

INTERVIEW WITH DR. BROOKE BAIR, DO

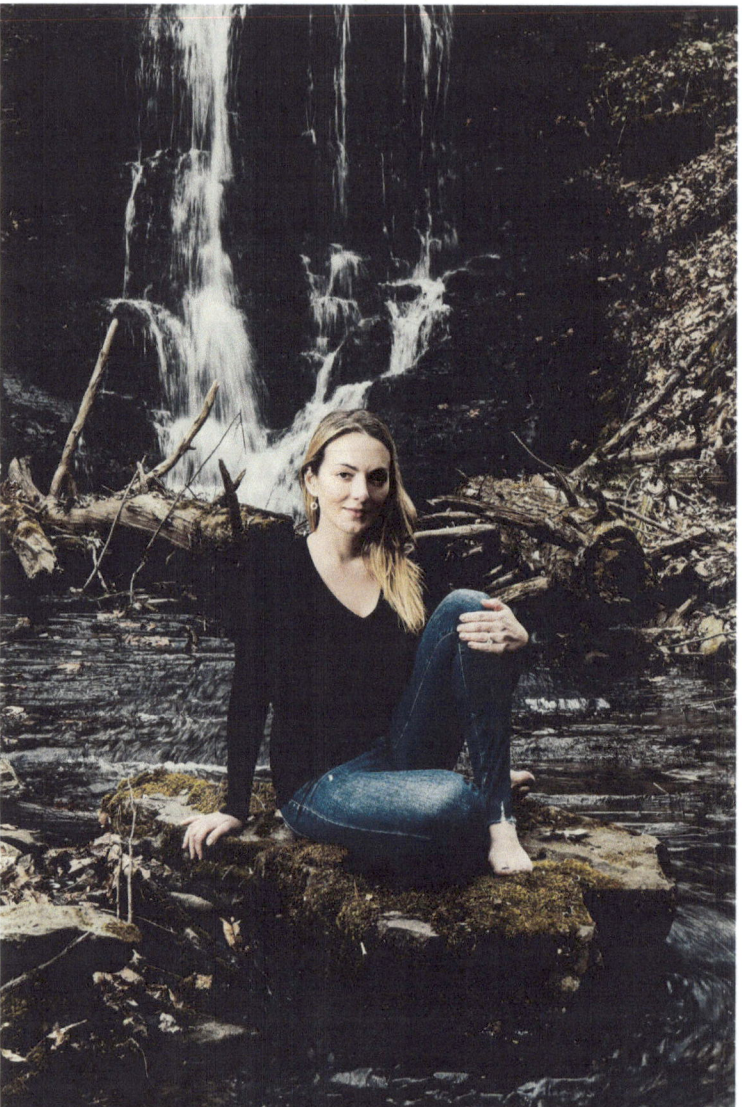

Maxwell: I imagine your (small) apartment living in the city had its own interesting twists. But today you showed me a picture of the big black bear right next to your house. That was awesome :) What is your favorite part of owning acreage of beautiful land with a creek, waterfalls and apparently a bear?

Dr. Bair: We love being outside together as a family. It's like a big playground. My daughter loves being outside and hiking. One of her favorite things to do is collect acorns :)

Being a mama-bear myself, I can't say I love that big furry animal so close to my house. I've been told they are easy to scare, but I'm not sure I ever want to find out.

Maxwell: Lip gloss and botox shots used to be very trendy in recent years. What is in style this spring?

Dr. Bair: Right now, I'm really embracing regenerative medicine and dermatology...

Maxwell: Clarify the jargon please... :)

Dr. Bair: As an Osteopathic physician, I was trained to believe there's more to good health than the absence of pain or disease. This whole-person approach to medicine focuses on prevention, helping promote the body's natural tendency toward health and self-healing. Regenerative medicine fits perfectly into the osteopathic philosophy of care.

One example of this in my practice is the use of PRP, or platelet-rich plasma. PRP is something that we obtain by taking a sample of the patients own blood and extracting the PRP, rich in growth factors that help to stimulate collagen formation. Stimulating collagen formation in the skin helps to eliminate deep and fine lines giving the skin a more plump and youthful appearance. Another example is using a micro-needling device called the Genius (by Lutronic) which delivers energy to deeper levels of the skin. This treatment helps with skin tightening, decreasing pore size, but also stimulates new collagen formation... so yet another way to get the body to do the "work" for you rather than inject foreign substances. We can actually use PRP and Genius together for some pretty amazing results, not just on the face, but the neck and body too.

Maxwell: Wow, never thought we'd go this high talking about style! Can I schedule an appointment now? Just kidding, I'll call your practice :) So what's ahead? What is your next big thing?

Dr. Bair: Well, after spring comes summer, and right now is the time when everyone has their eyes set on summer (and ending the quarantine). The big thing right now is going to be Coolsculpting. This is a treatment that will kick your summer body countdown into high gear and get rid of the exercise-resistant bulges. permanently! Coolsculpting is also a form of regenerative medicine, and the technology behind the treatment is really amazing. During the treatment, the temperature of the fat cell is lowered (hence the name COOLsculpting) which is basically a cellular injury. Then our lymphatic system clears those injured fat cells from the body. Our body is naturally clearing thousands of "injured" or unhealthy cells every day. Coolsculpting in a way just redirects the body's efforts to focus on areas of stubborn and unwanted fat.

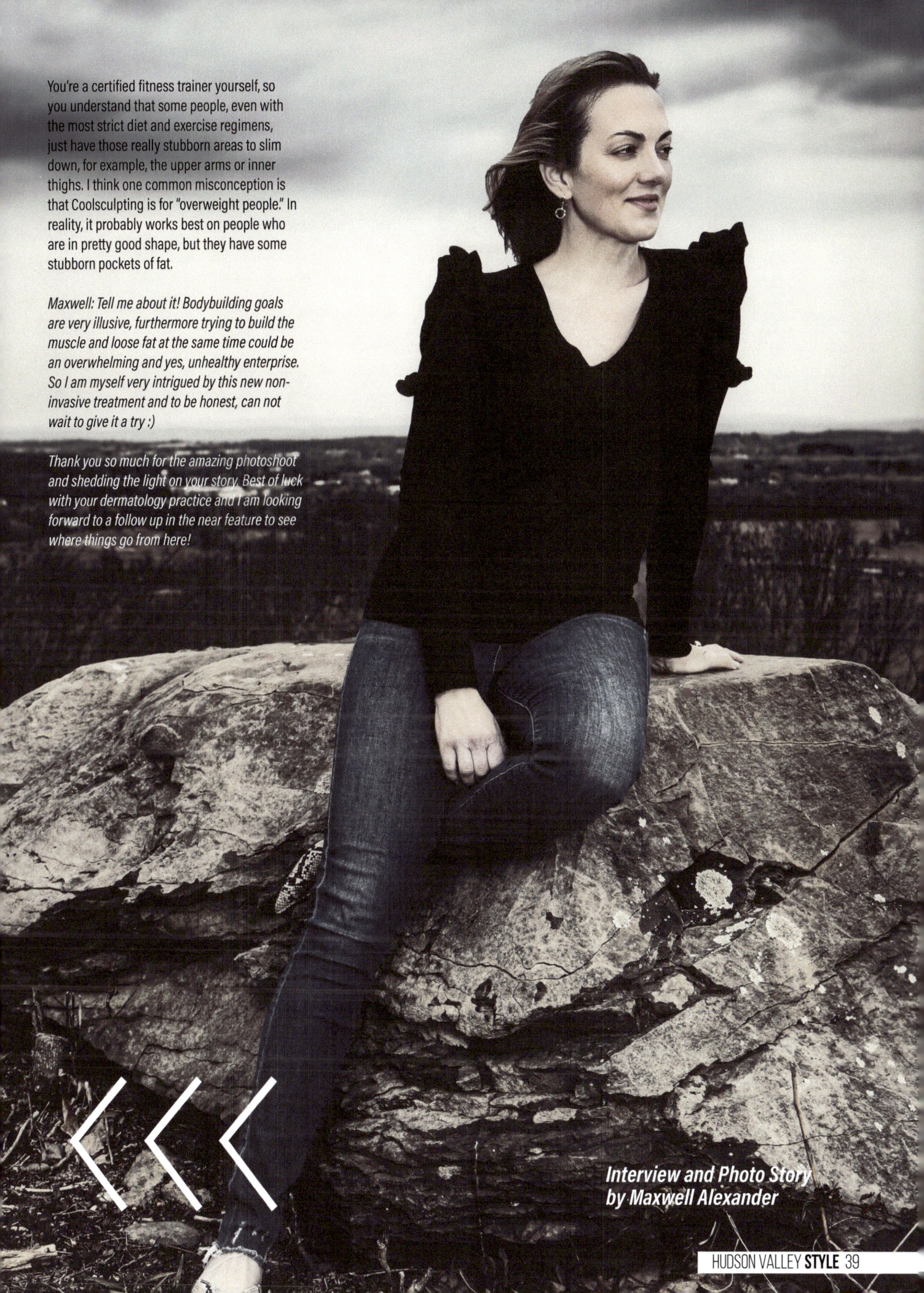

You're a certified fitness trainer yourself, so you understand that some people, even with the most strict diet and exercise regimens, just have those really stubborn areas to slim down, for example, the upper arms or inner thighs. I think one common misconception is that Coolsculpting is for "overweight people." In reality, it probably works best on people who are in pretty good shape, but they have some stubborn pockets of fat.

Maxwell: Tell me about it! Bodybuilding goals are very illusive, furthermore trying to build the muscle and loose fat at the same time could be an overwhelming and yes, unhealthy enterprise. So I am myself very intrigued by this new non-invasive treatment and to be honest, can not wait to give it a try :)

Thank you so much for the amazing photoshoot and shedding the light on your story. Best of luck with your dermatology practice and I am looking forward to a follow up in the near feature to see where things go from here!

Interview and Photo Story by Maxwell Alexander

REAL ESTATE PHOTOGRAPHY 101

61% MORE VIEWS ONLINE WITH PROFESSIONAL PHOTOS

UP TO 47% HIGHER ASKING PRICE/SQFT

80% OF BUYERS CITED THEY WOULDN'T EVEN CONSIDER A LISTING WITHOUT PHOTOGRAPHS

98% OF BUYERS THINK PROFESSIONAL PHOTOS ARE MOST USEFUL WHEN LOOKING FOR HOME ONLINE

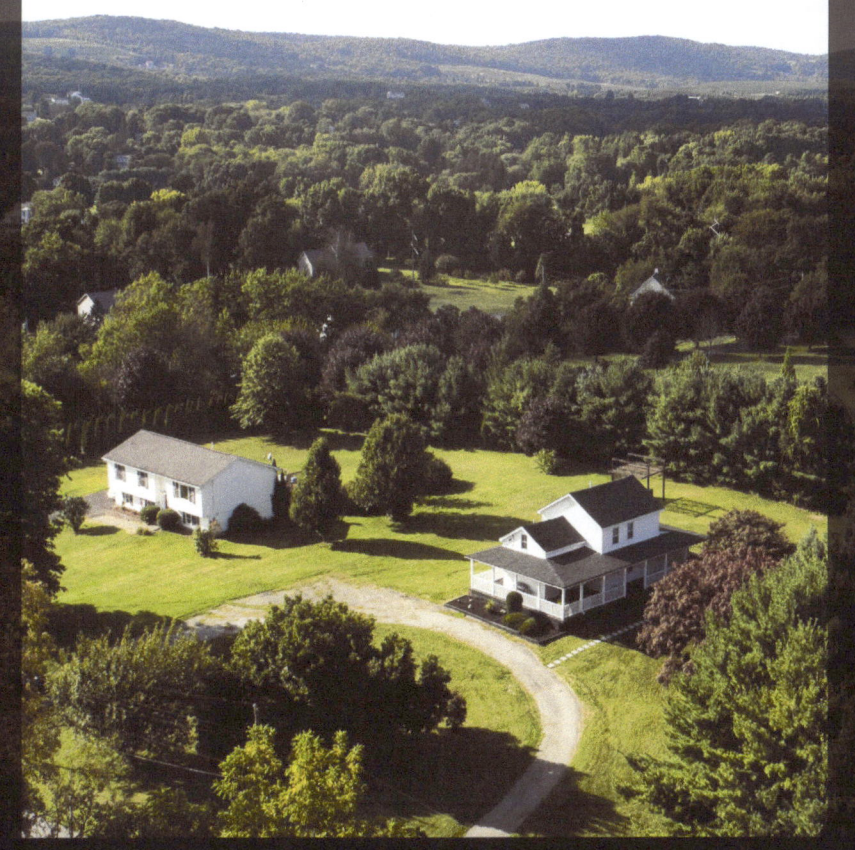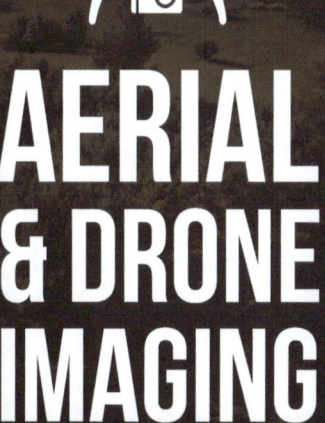

AERIAL & DRONE IMAGING

CONSIDER THESE HIGH-TECH UPGRADES

DUNCANAVENUE™
HUDSON VALLEY REAL ESTATE SERVICES

SCHEDULE YOUR PHOTOSHOOT @
DUNCANAVENUE.COM

STATISTICS SOURCE:
NATIONAL ASSOCIATION OF REALTORS

PROFESSIONAL LIGHTING

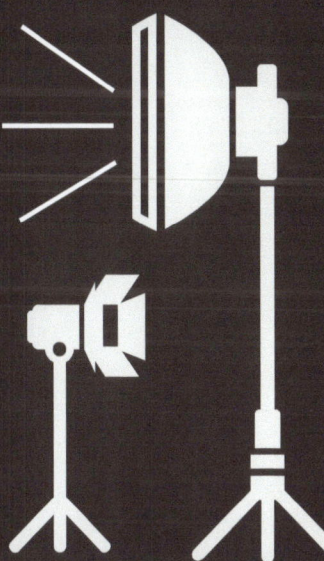

DSLR CAMERAS & LENSES

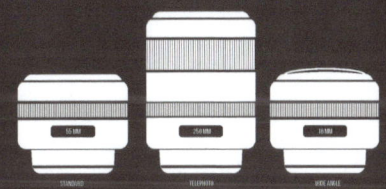
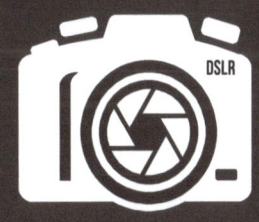

PROFESSIONAL RETOUCHING

+ DIGITAL STAGING

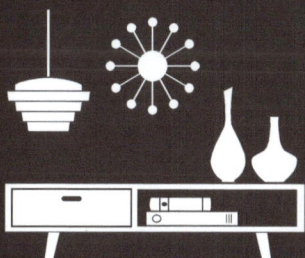

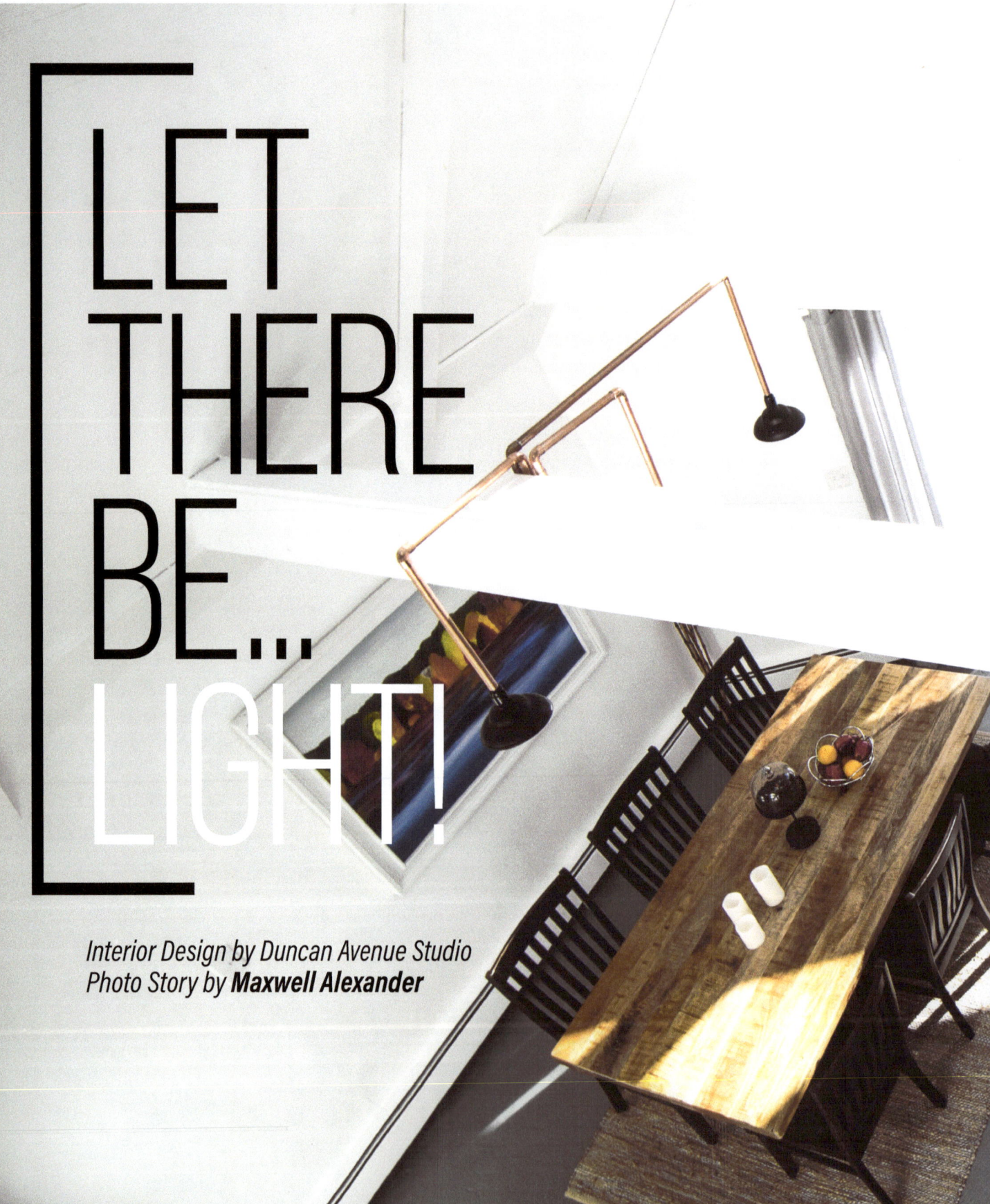

[HUDSON VALLEY STYLE LIVING]

LET THERE BE... LIGHT!

Interior Design by Duncan Avenue Studio
Photo Story by **Maxwell Alexander**

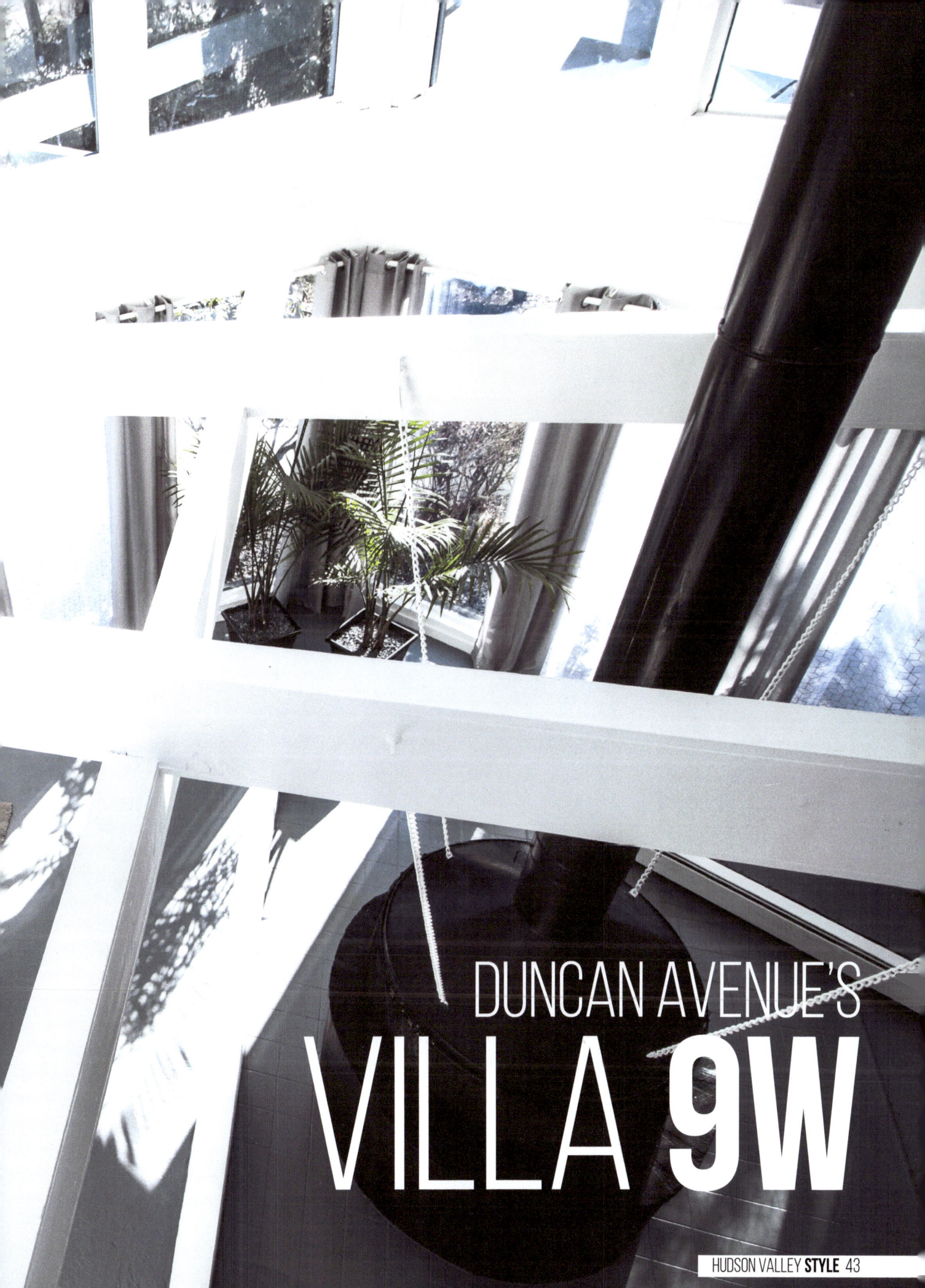

DUNCAN AVENUE'S VILLA 9W

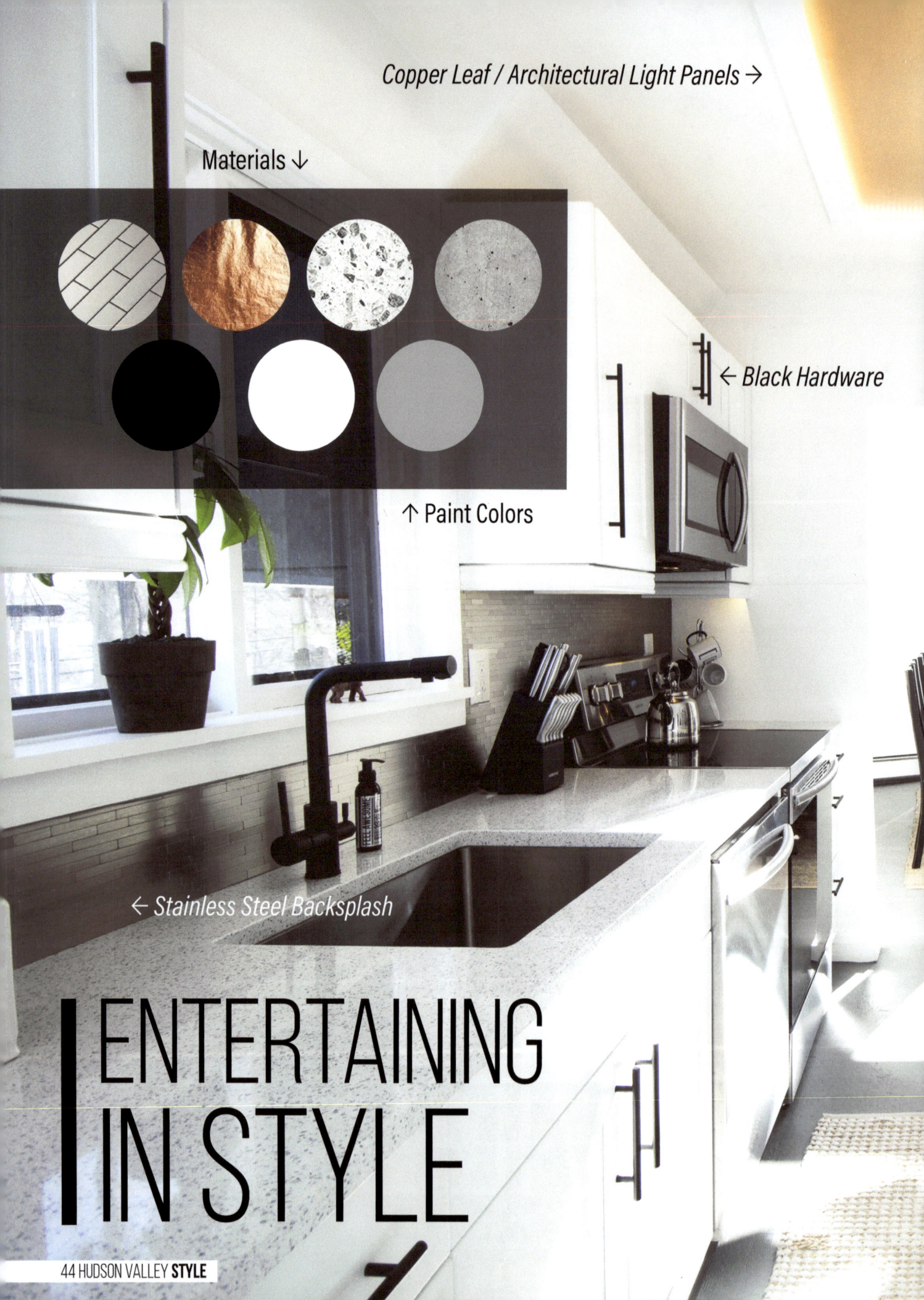

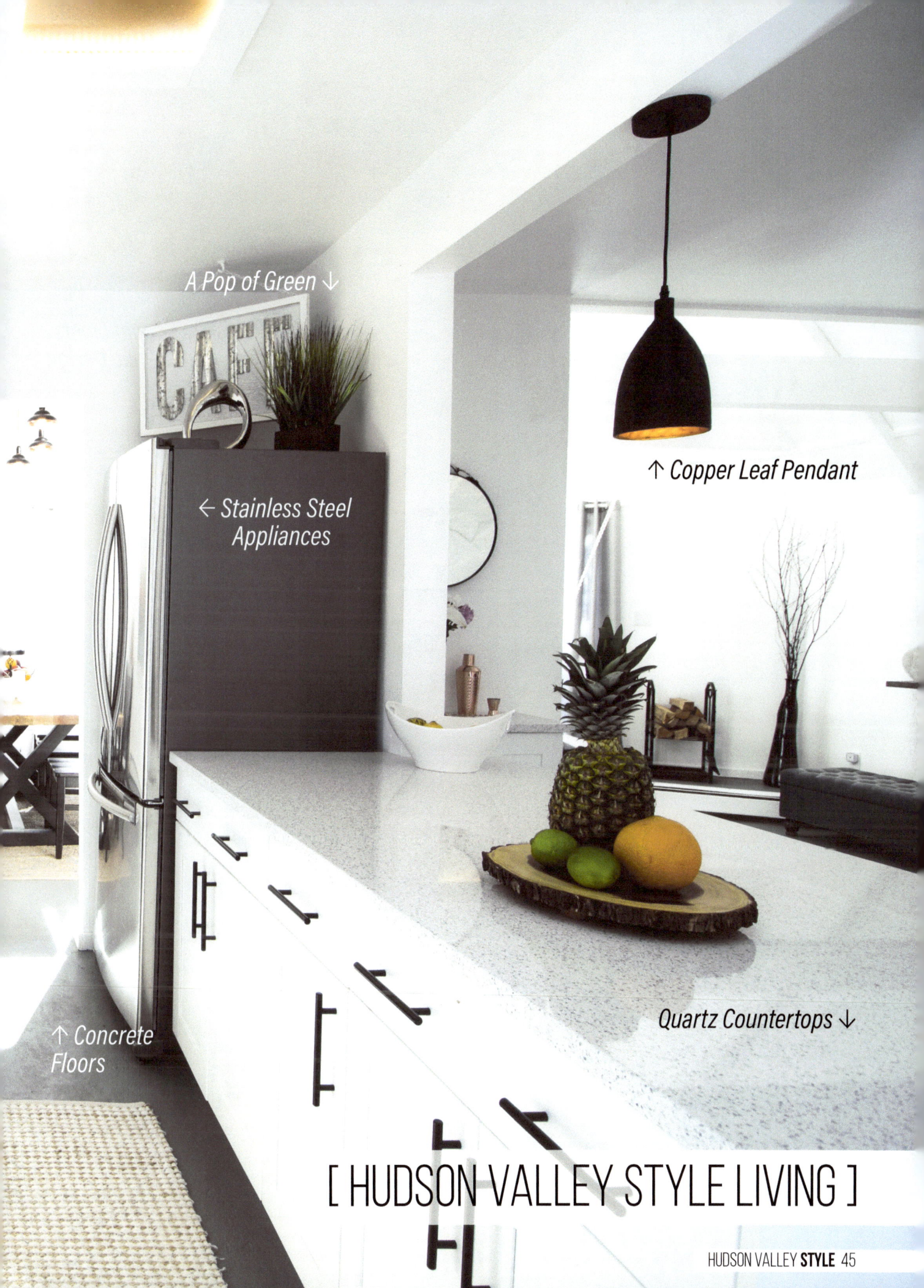

[HUDSON VALLEY STYLE LIVING]

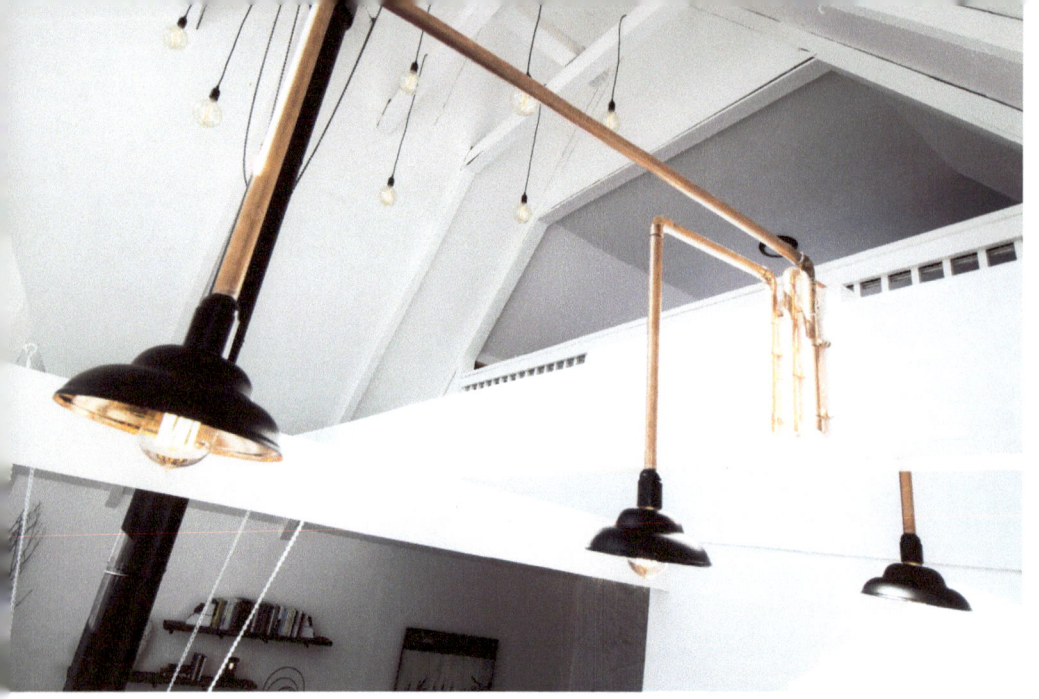

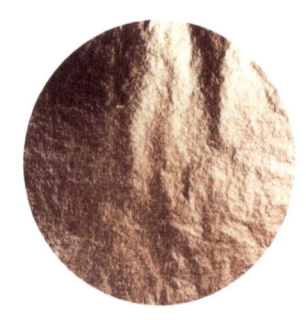

← *Custom Copper Lights*
© *Duncan Avenue Design*

White Granite Wall →

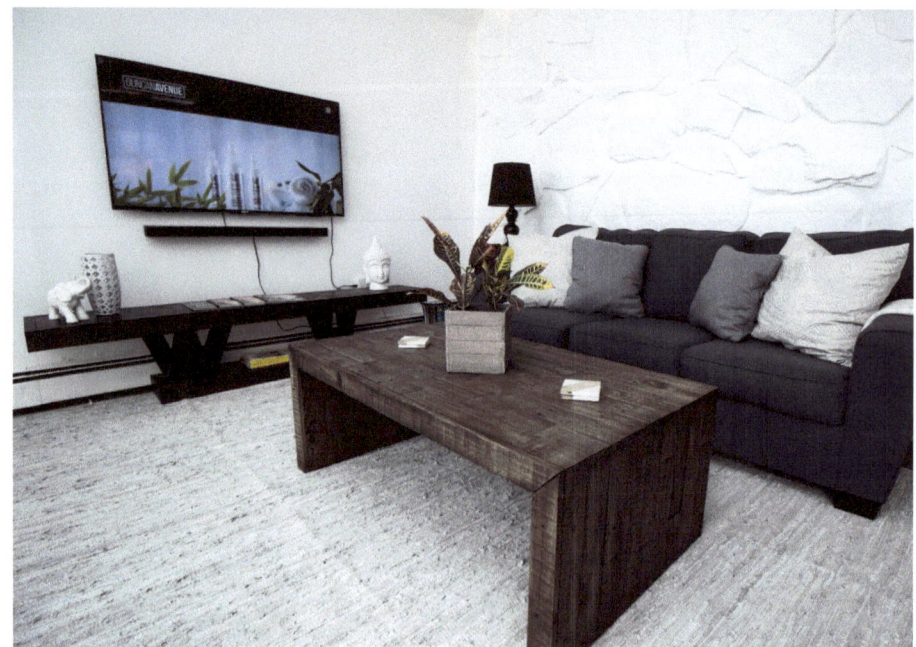

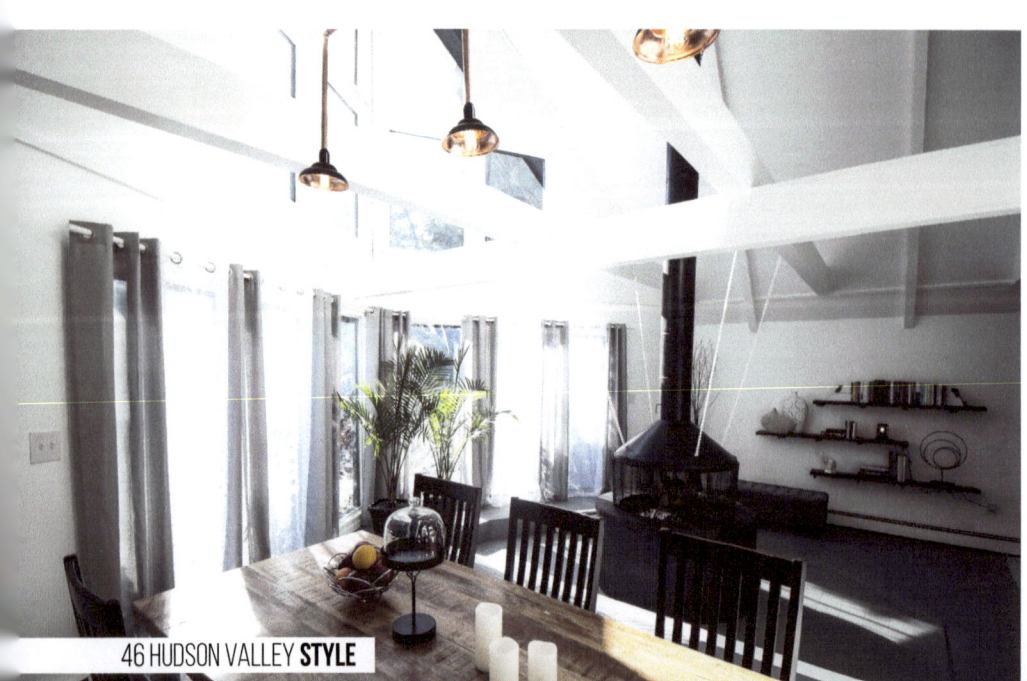

Wood Accents →

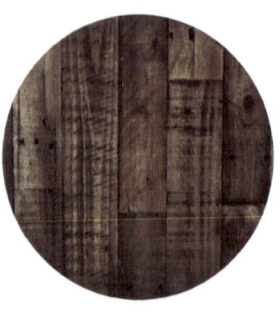

← *Formal Dining Area*

LIVING SPACE | WHITE BALANCE

Custom Entertainment
↓ *Console*

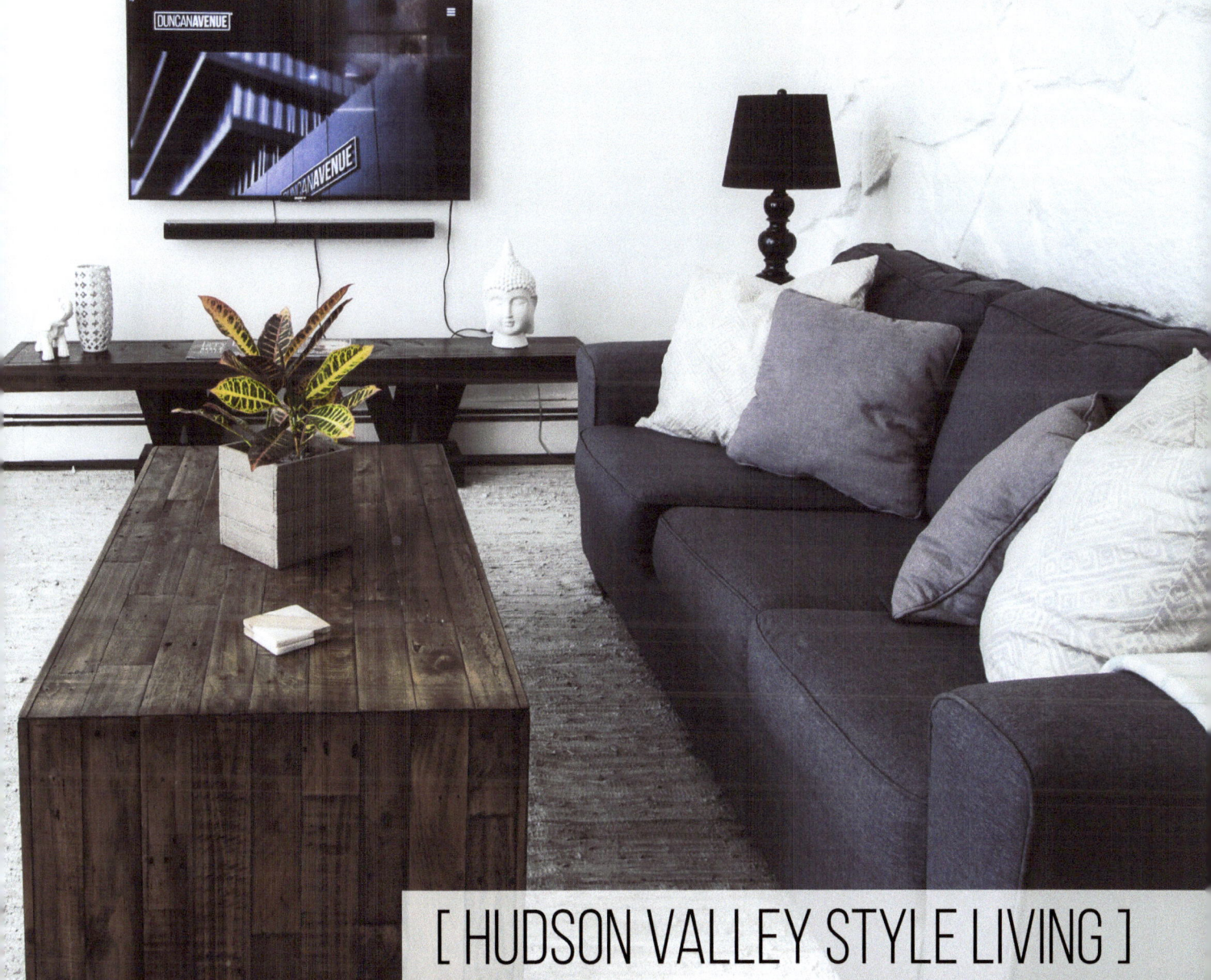

[HUDSON VALLEY STYLE LIVING]

[da-aromatherapy.com]

KEEP NATURE NATURAL.

Our Natural Insect Repellents are made with Organic Essential Oils and are free of chemical pesticides that are harmful to your health and the environment.

da aromatherapy™

FIVE MISTAKES THAT CAN RUIN YOUR FAT LOSS PLAN

by Certified Bodybuilding Trainer Maxwell Alexander

Every year, millions of people across the world attempt to lose weight. Many of them fail. If you would like to give your weight loss plan the best possible chance of success, you should try to avoid making any of the common mistakes that cause others to fail, such as:

NOT EATING ENOUGH

When attempting to shed those extra pounds, you may be tempted to skip meals or avoid eating for extended periods of time. Unfortunately, this approach is only likely to result in you feeling grumpy, lethargic, and desperate for a snack later in the day. To improve your odds of weight loss success, try to eat a healthy meal three times a day.

SETTING UNREALISTIC GOALS

As you begin your weight loss journey, you should set some goals for yourself. In doing so, however, you should ensure that your targets are attainable. If you set goals that are impossible to achieve, you are likely to feel down and unmotivated when you inevitably fail to meet them. As a result, you may decide to give up on your weight loss plan entirely.

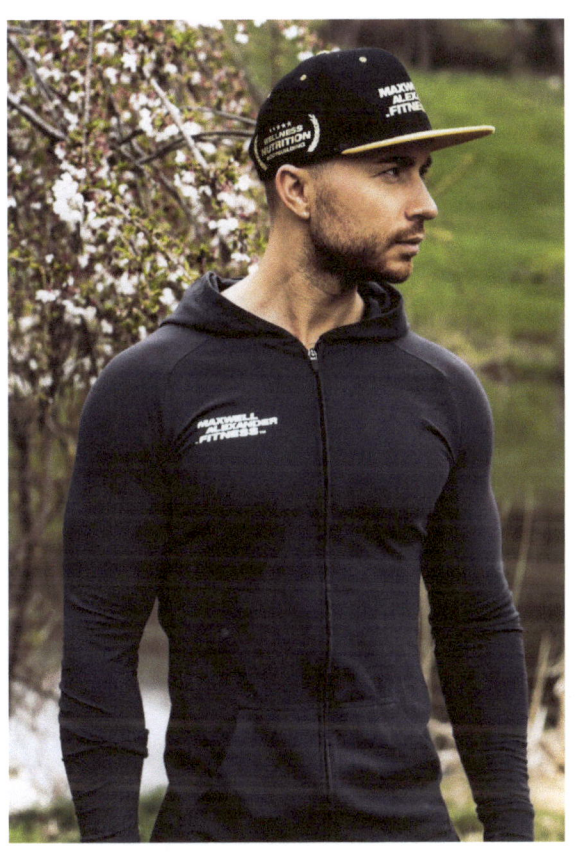

FAILING TO REWARD YOURSELF

As you accomplish your weight loss goals, you should take a moment to reward yourself for all your hard work. Of course, you should try to avoid using food as a reward. Instead, consider opting for new clothes or even a short vacation.

DOING THE SAME EXERCISES EVERY DAY

Exercising regularly can be a great way to lose some weight and improve your fitness. However, you should avoid becoming overly reliant on any one particular form of exercise. If your workouts are the same every day, you are likely to get bored of them very quickly. To keep yourself interested and engaged, mix up your exercise plan as much as possible.

NOT GETTING ENOUGH SLEEP

When it comes to weight loss, sleep has many benefits. First and foremost, it provides your body with a chance to recover from the rigors of the day, something which is particularly useful if you have an intense workout schedule. It also re-energizes you for the following day and can speed up your metabolism. In short, if you are not getting enough shuteye, you are likely to find it difficult to lose weight.

IN CLOSING

Losing weight can be challenging. However, it does not have to be impossible. As long as you keep working hard and avoid making the mistakes outlined above, you should notice those extra pounds begin to drop off before too long. If you still need help, I have an awesome Weight Loss Program just for you! Working with one of the Best Online Fitness Coaches like myself, you can get better results in a shorter period of time, so why not give it a try? Log on to MaxwellAlexander.Fitness to learn more about my Online Weight Loss Coaching Program.

The way people buy and sell things has inherently changed in the last decade. Why should real estate be any different? The industry as you know it is lagging dreadfully behind, but Almax Realty is disrupting the system with a bold, new outlook on what is necessary to become a successful real estate agent.

CUTTING-EDGE ENVIRONMENT

Contrary to the notion that we're all lazy and entitled, Millennials are overtaking the workforce and the real estate market. Alexander Maxwell Realty understands your need for a cutting-edge environment to thrive in. We're not talking about gimmicks like bean bags and espresso bars; we are talking about a technology-powered system designed for agents that operate differently—a system that enables you to succeed.

THE OPPORTUNITY IS IN THE FIELD

As a matter of fact, the less you see our office, the better, even though it's a beautiful office. We do not require you to waste time on senseless, hierarchical office duties because the opportunity is in the field. You get what you put in, and with a flexible schedule that allows you to work as much or as little as you'd like, not a minute is wasted. Our agency is not the old boy's club that you know so well. We think of ourselves as business partners, providing you with all the tools it takes to go from showing to closing, to an unrivaled commission check in your bank account.

WORLD-CLASS MARKETING

At Almax Realty, our agents are always moving forward. Our commission structure is based on a true buyer's agent 90-10 split, with no extra charges or fees. We are not in the business of thievery. We strive to invest in our agents from day one by providing honest commission for honest work, and an arsenal of world-class marketing materials to help you build strong client relationships. From complimentary, strategic marketing packages to award-winning photography, we have your back.

CONTROL YOUR DESTINY

Alexander Maxwell Realty is a platform where you control your destiny and your career, and we want to do everything we can to help you reach your goals. Support and innovation are the pillars on which that platform lies, and our core values transcend the hollow text on a mission statement. We have a growing team of highly motivated, like-minded agents and we are always looking for more, so just drop us a line to get started!

LEARN MORE & APPLY TO JOIN AT ALMAXREALTY.COM

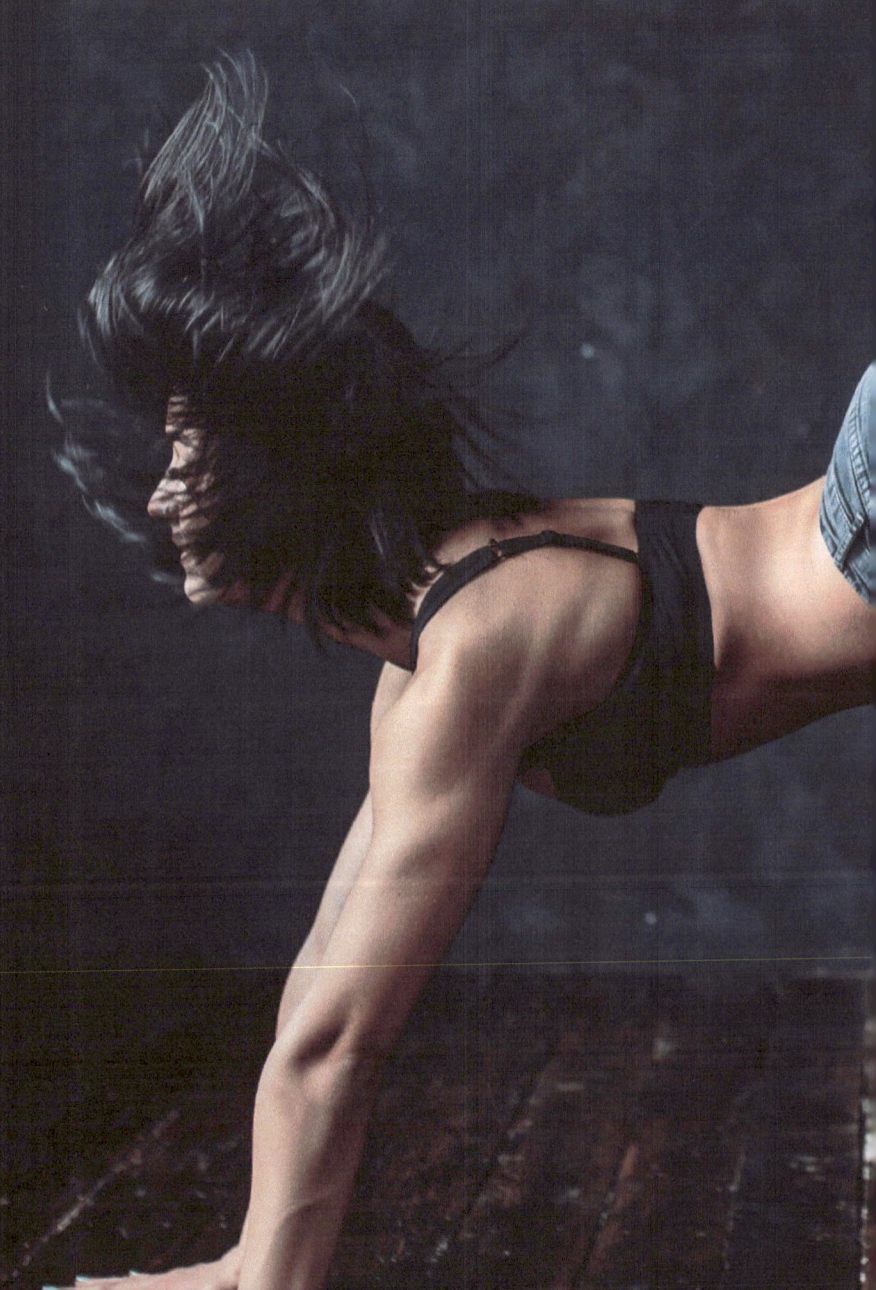

#FRESH
#AMBITIOUS
#VICTORIOUS
#JOINUS

[REAL ESTATE STYLE]

JOIN HUDSON VALLEY'S BEST REAL ESTATE AGENCY

BY DINO ALEXANDER
CEO, ALEXANDER MAXWELL REALTY

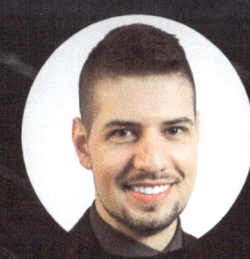

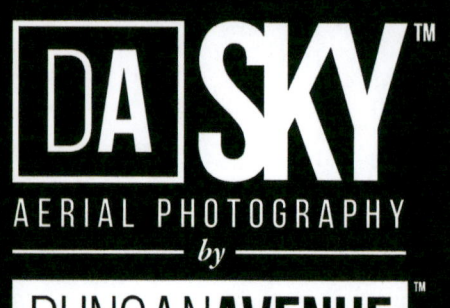

SPRING ESSENTIALS

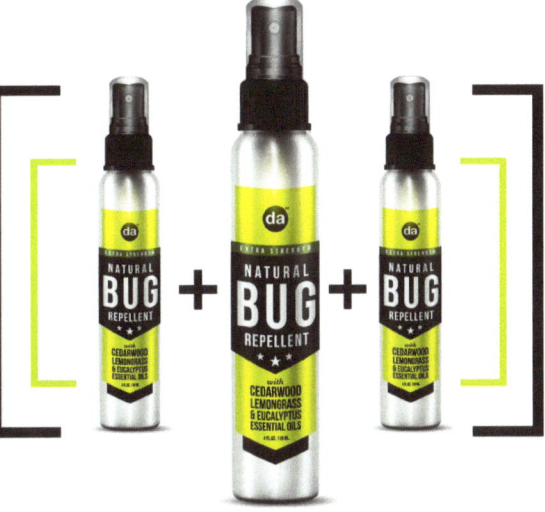

WOODLAND TRAILS BLEND
by DA Aromatherapy Collection

This natural insect repellent is made with 7 organic essential oils, it provides broad-spectrum protection and repels mosquitoes and ticks, fleas and many other pesky insects. The Best Natural Tick and Mosquito Repellent Spray is created for direct skin contact, safe for Humans and Pets and featuring exclusive Woodland Trails™ blend of Organic Lemongrass, Eucalyptus Lemon, and Eucalyptus Globulus, Cedarwood (Cedar Oil), Rosemary, Clove, and Lavender Essential Oils.

Our signature Tick and Mosquito Natural Spray will keep you sting and bite-free without the use of pesticides that are harmful to humans, the environment at large and especially good insects like honeybees. Our natural tick and mosquito repellent can help to protect you when sprayed in a room, on the balcony, in a car, on the body, and even on your clothes without staining.

DA-AROMATHERAPY.COM

$17.00

INSPIRING AROMATHERAPY MIST WITH ORGANIC LAVENDER AND SANDALWOOD ESSENTIAL OILS - WINDS OF STORMKING™
by DA Aromatherapy Collection

A luxurious and sensual fragrance of rich, woodsy sandalwood accord and beautiful flowery notes of lavender and spice. Winds of Stormking™ Essential Oil Blend perfectly captures the cool mountain breezes, sun sparkles in the Hudson River waters and lush foliage of the Hudson Valley.

DA-AROMATHERAPY.COM

$9.00

NATURAL HAND SANITIZERS WITH ORGANIC ESSENTIAL OILS
by DA Aromatherapy Collection

Working out at the gym or taking a Savasana on your yoga mat? Protect yourself and loved ones plus get an aromatherapy boost on the go with these natural hand sanitizers. DA Aromatherapy Hand Sanitizing Mists with Organic Essential Oils are effective against 99.9% of common germs and bacteria.

DA-AROMATHERAPY.COM

$9.00

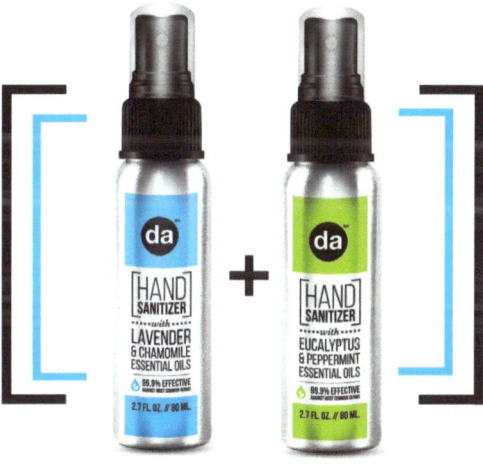

LOVE IS IN THE AIR

54 HUDSON VALLEY **STYLE**

"LOVE IS IN THE AIR"
CAMPAIGN FOR ETHNOLOVE ACCESSORIES
CREATIVE DIRECTOR @LENA.GERGERDT
STYLE @MARINA_WELZ
MUAH ALEXANDRA LIKSCHIN
PHOTOGRAPHY @ALLA_RODIONOVA_FOTOGRAF
MODEL @ANASTASIA_MOHYLNA

"LOVE IS IN THE AIR"
PHOTO STORY BY ALLA RODIONOVA

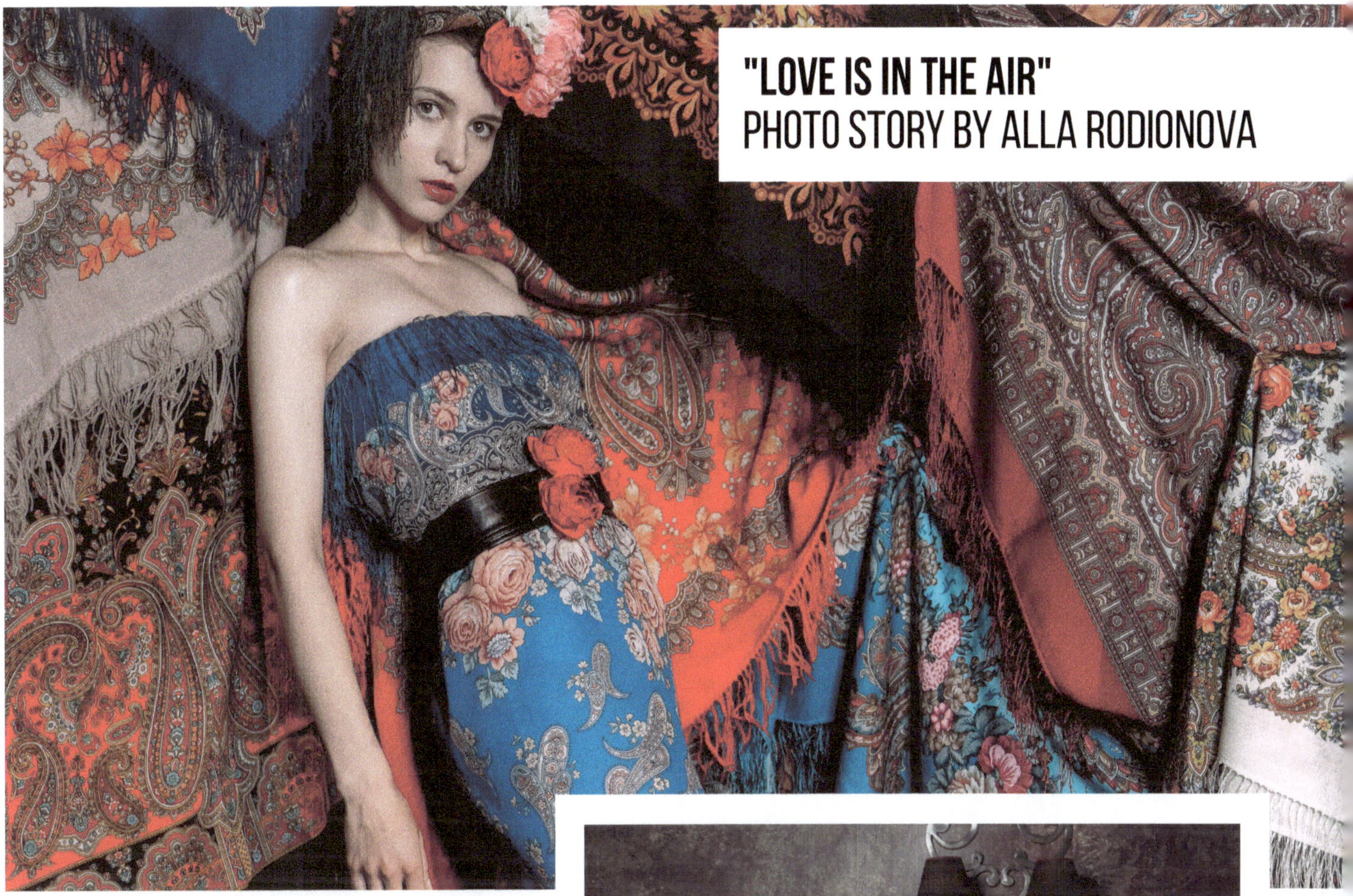

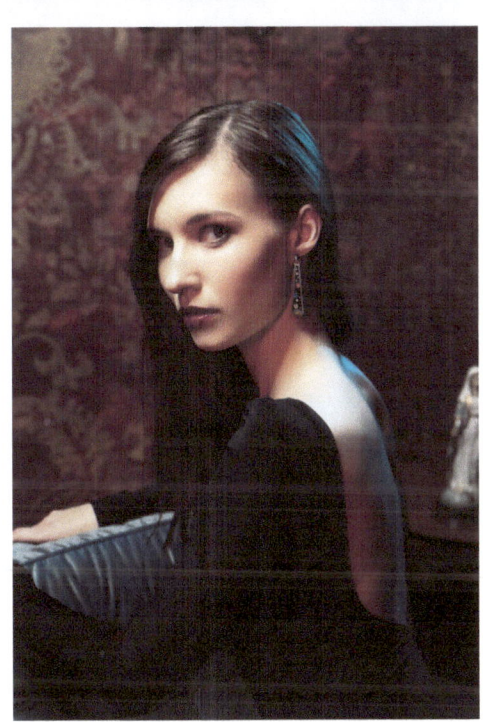
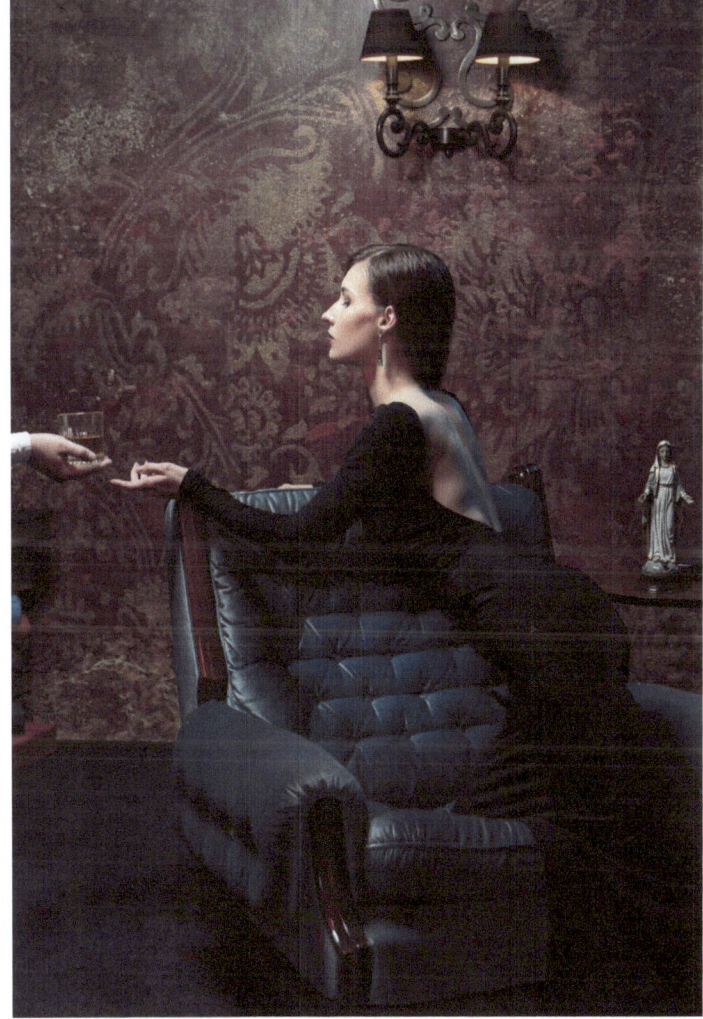

#REAL
#PROVOCATIVE
#STYLE

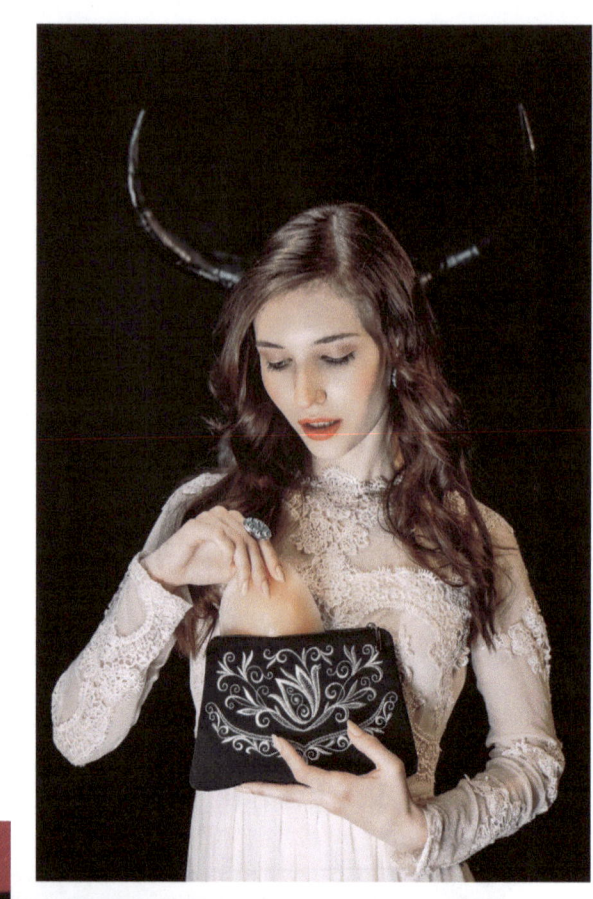

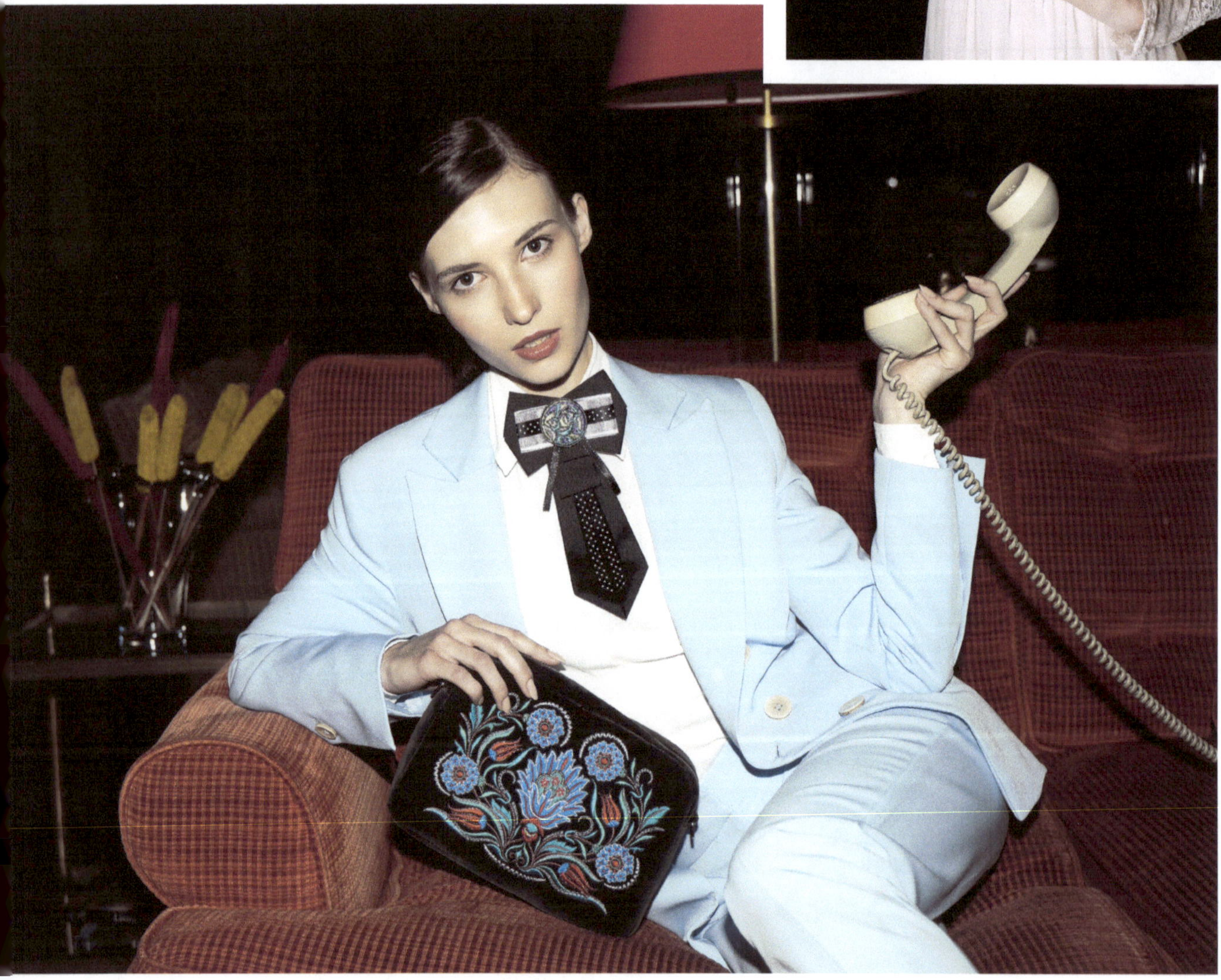

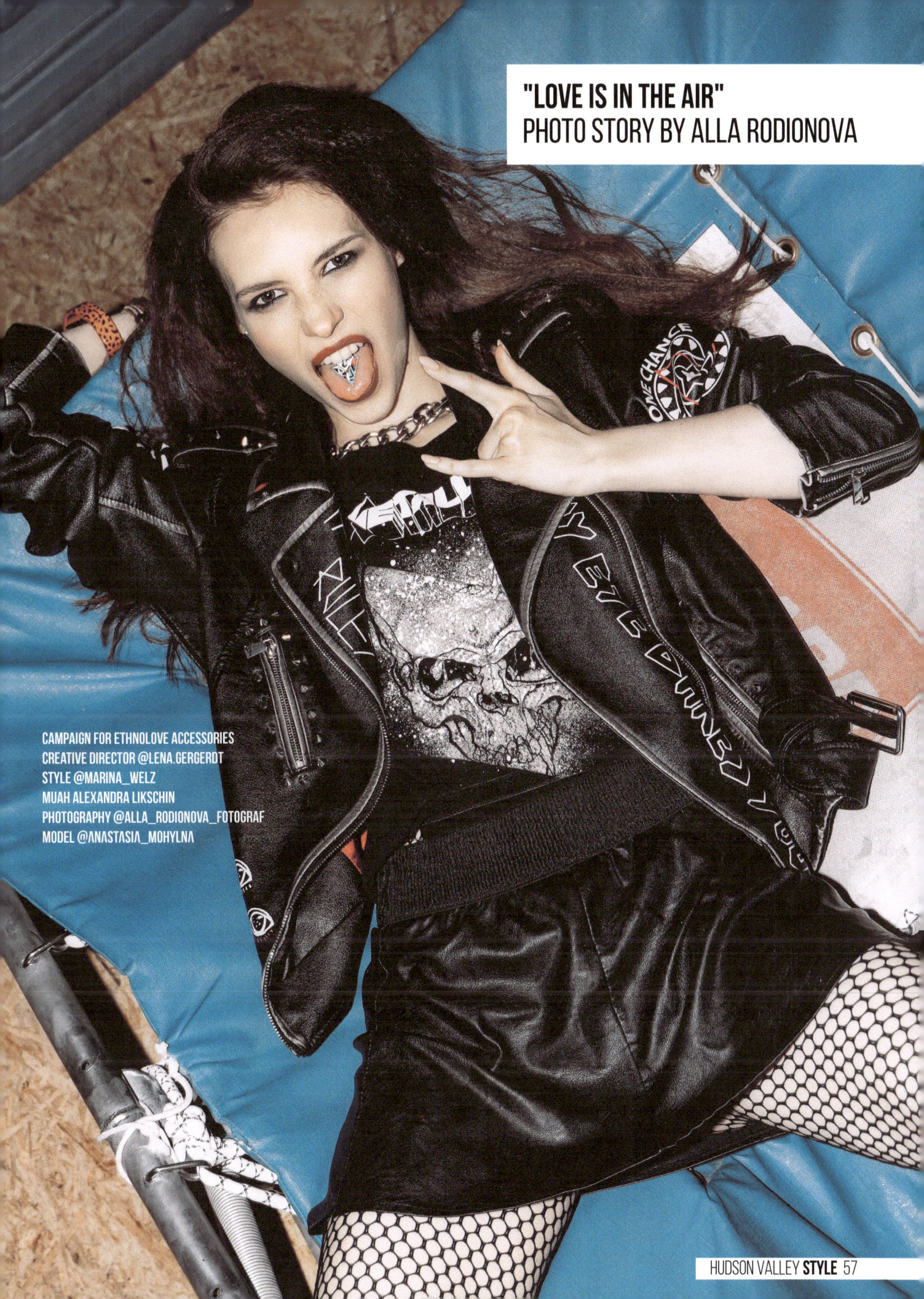

TO STAGE, OR NOT TO STAGE?

Learn More about this design project →
at duncanavenue.com/design

STAGED HOMES SELL 79% FASTER

STAGED HOMES SOLD IN 11 DAYS OR LESS
ON AVERAGE SPEND **73% LESS TIME ON THE MARKET**
COMPARED TO AVERAGE 60 DAYS ON THE MARKET

81% OF BUYERS
FIND THAT STAGING HELPS THEM BETTER **VISUALIZE** A PROPERTY AS THEIR **FUTURE HOME**

HIGHER SALES PRICES
STAGED HOMES SELL FOR **17% MORE** THAN NON-STAGED HOMES

BUYERS MOST OFTEN offer 1%-5% increase on the REAL VALUE OF A STAGED HOME

SELLERS SPEND LESS THAN 1% FOR STAGING SERVICES to get a 1000% RETURN ON INVESTMENT

HOME STAGING CAN BOOST PERCEIVED VALUE OF A HOME BY 20%

95% OF BUYER'S AGENTS SAY THAT HOME STAGING HAS A POSITIVE EFFECT ON THE HOME BUYER'S VIEW OF THE PROPERTY

3% YET LESS THAN 3% OF HOMES LISTED ON MLS ARE STAGED

DUNCAN AVENUE
HUDSON VALLEY REAL ESTATE SERVICES

SCHEDULE YOUR CONSULTATION @
DUNCANAVENUE.COM

STATISTICS SOURCE:
NATIONAL ASSOCIATION OF REALTORS

1-YEAR ONLINE BODYBUILDING PROGRAM

DESIGNER ★ ★ BODY ™

MAXWELL ALEXANDER .FITNESS

TECHNOLOGY-POWERED 24/7 TRAINING
1-Year Online or In-Person Bodybuilding Program

START YOUR JOURNEY TODAY!
Sign up at **MaxwellAlexander.Fitness**

www.ingramcontent.com/pod-product-compliance
Lightning Source LLC
Chambersburg PA
CBHW051210220526
45473CB00003B/978